A JOHN CATT PUBLICATION

ANDY SAM

THE
COMPASSIONATE
TEACHER

Why compassion should be
at the heart of our schools

First Published 2019

by John Catt Educational Ltd,
15 Riduna Park, Station Road
Melton, Woodbridge IP12 1QT

Tel: +44 (0) 1394 389850
Email: enquiries@johncatt.com
Website: www.johncatt.com

ISBN: 978 1 912906 03 1

Set and designed by John Catt Educational Limited

Reviews

Well researched and practical, this book shows you why and how compassion should be placed at the heart of schools. What shines through is Andy's warmth and humanity – two qualities our education system desperately needs. A remarkable read.

Adrian Bethune
Bestselling Amazon author and teacher

Reading this book inspires me to imagine how the classroom will be when emotional intelligence meets pedagogy. Transformation in schools begins here. A school improvement must-read.

This is a seminal book. Only when well-being is at the heart of our education system will schools yield consistent and sustained success.

Jill Brennan
Founder of Using Visualisation and educational consultant

A deeply personal individual account of teaching and the importance of building courage to be truly compassionate to yourself. A powerful read.

Dame Alison Peacock
Chief Executive of The Charted College of Teaching

This is a book that every teacher who has ever felt under pressure and exhausted should read. In it, you will find plenty of guidance to help you achieve greater balance and adopt fresh perspectives on what should undoubtedly be one of the most rewarding professions around.

Douglas Wise
Assistant headteacher

An important contribution to the discussion about mental health: a gripping account of one professional's journey into the abyss and the remarkable people and resources which helped him through. It is a testament to his tenacity that he writes about this in unsparing detail and frames his recovery within the wider research literature. There will be many of us who have had similar experiences or have witnessed a loved one go through a version of this. And there will be many people working in schools who will be grateful that this book has been written.

Mary Myatt
Education writer, adviser and speaker

Andy's book begins with an honest and courageous discussion of his own mental health challenges, and goes on to explain how compassion-focused therapy has been, and continues to be, crucial to his recovery.

This is a warm, reflective exploration of the nature of compassion and empathy, and the importance of paying attention and offering care, both to yourself and to others. Andy draws on his extensive reading and also on interviews with counselling professionals, medical and mental health professionals and pioneers, and educators of all types, including academics, classroom practitioners and leaders. This helps to ground the discussion of the power of CFT in the reality of human experience, especially with respect to the world of education and the 'threat' posed by its current pressures.

The book offers suggestions of practical strategies to safeguard our well-being and increase our professional effectiveness as we build our self-awareness and the most positive, constructive relationships, showing compassion towards ourselves, our colleagues, our students, in our teaching and even in our marking. It also offers helpful suggestions for further reading for those who wish to delve more deeply into the theory and underlying principles relating to CFT.

I absolutely endorse Andy's key message:

> *'If we want education to be successful,*
> *we have to look after the people in it.'*

Jill Berry
Former head, now leadership consultant

Acknowledgements

Thank you to all the incredible people that have given up their time and shared their thoughts with me: it has been a pleasure to speak with each and every one of you. There is so, so much to be hopeful about in education, and it is because of the truly wonderful people we have in the profession.

My proofreaders have been incredible too: Mum, Dad, Dr Philippa Sammons (my darling wife), Dr Natalie Jewitt, Jill Berry, Holly Wildman and Doug Wise have been supportive and encouraging, lifting me up whenever I needed a boost and a reminder that what I was doing was valid and worthwhile.

Last – but not least – thank you to my own inner voice: I acknowledge you; I recognise you; you are a part of me, but you do not define me.

For Flippy and Wilf – for giving me my drive and my soothe.

And for Mum, Dad and Matt – for rallying and being there when I needed you.

Gemma and John – you are exceptional people.

Contents

Foreword

Last year, my wife and I had our first child. Like many earnest first-time parents, we have spent considerable time discussing and debating what kind of little boy we want to raise. As an economist and an English teacher, we haven't always reached a consensus, particularly in terms of his possible future career prospects (I am regimentally sticking with the 'Future Shakespeare' plan!)

There is, however, one quality and virtue that we wholeheartedly agreed on: we want him to be a compassionate individual. It is the value that is often neglected in conversations about how best to live our lives, or how best to encourage others to live theirs. It is simple in its intentions, yet much more challenging in its execution: to be able to recognise and sympathise with our own suffering and that of others.

And, as Andy Sammons illuminates in this important and courageous book, compassion is a value that is often sadly neglected in our modern schools.

With an accountability system's obsession with data and spreadsheets now often more valued than relationships, work-life balance in tatters and a ubiquitous mental health crisis, there is an urgent need for a return to a more humane vision of education. Without it, we will see more and more exhausted and stressed teachers flooding to leave a profession that has failed to offer the hopeful promise of 'making a difference'.

Andy is all too aware of how all-encompassing and damaging it is trying to function in such toxic school environments. Sometimes we need to hit the bottom in order to find the strength and conviction to reassess our lives, and that has certainly been his experience. In *The Compassionate Teacher*, Andy provides his readers with a brave and honest portrayal of his own breakdown and struggles with mental health.

His candid journey to find a healthier relationship with his own thoughts, and indeed to rediscover compassion for himself, is what gives his book an authenticity and makes it vital reading for anyone involved in education. He is driven by a passion to share his deep understanding of both psychology and well-being in order to prevent what is far too common in our profession: burnout and exhaustion.

Andy's message is simple and important: no matter how much we may outwardly appear to effectively manage our emotions, we all need to be aware of a toolkit of strategies to help us cope with stress. It starts with looking at ourselves; after all, how can we look after the welfare of young people unless we can prioritise our own well-being?

Developing a more positive and optimistic approach to our work involves honing our compassionate voice and stepping away from an endless inner narrative of negativity. Instead, with Andy's sage guidance we learn to be more aware of our thought patterns and how to recognise when they are inhibiting us, rather than leading to positive actions. There is also practical guidance about how we take more ownership over that most elusive of qualities: a work-life balance.

As vital as this examination is, this is not just a book that will improve our own well-being and arm us with an ability to cope with the many stresses of teaching. Andy also provides a strategic roadmap for improving the system based on rediscovering the space for compassion and warmth. It deliberately refutes the quick-fix systems that often dominate in education, instead examining why compassion could be the key to all our educational futures. It is not one that negates high expectations, but it illuminates how dialogue and allowing space for reflection and listening will enable positive change.

The wide range of important and informed voices that Andy has interviewed add to the urgency of the narrative and his philosophy for positive change. Supported by the words of our most impressive educational leaders and mental health experts, Andy's own message about the unique potential of collaboration in education is powerfully expressed within the pages of his book. Together, these voices powerfully chorus the need for change and how we can achieve it, on both a personal and systematic level.

The Compassionate Teacher recognises that schools are hugely complex places, in which the interpersonal needs are significant and varied. Far too often, we are all on autopilot – too busy to recognise the human needs around us. Andy's guidance on simply focusing on improving our ability to listen and nurture each other can recapture the joy of working in schools.

With our colleagues, even something as nuanced and complex as providing lesson feedback can be visibly improved by adopting the compassion model. We have all experienced management and guidance that channels our passion, an individual that makes us feel like a genuine person and someone who matters – rather than a functional cog in a soulless machine. Our work and motivation is visibly enhanced when we know we are trusted and treated with this compassion. Andy offers a multitude of ways to improve our ability to recognise others, partly by simply rediscovering our need to collaborate and work together, rather than being pitted against each other.

Then there is what matters most to all of us: our relationships with our students and what happens in our classrooms. Andy's section on compassionate teaching provides practical and informed guidance on how to sustain effective relationships, and have real impact in our lessons. It is clear that Andy is a deeply reflective and passionate classroom practitioner, and approaching his teaching through a compassionate lens has had a transformative impact. It is all layered again through a very human level: with honesty and warmth at the core of our classrooms, the conditions for learning are significantly developed.

Reading Andy's book is a timely reminder of the reasons teachers want to enter the profession in the first place: a profound desire to do something positive with our lives and to have a genuine impact. At its core is a moral drive and the integrity to make our profession kinder and more optimistic again. As he acknowledges in his conclusions, there is a recurrent thread running through *The Compassionate Teacher*: reclaiming our profession.

So, in terms of nurturing: what do I want my little boy to develop? The same as I want for the people I work with, and indeed for myself: compassion for himself, for others and for the world around him. This vital and important book could well be the fuel to spark a rediscovery of those values in our schools, and in doing so make our profession more humane and joyful again. Reading this book will make you want to join him in loudly exclaiming the transformative power compassion could have in our schools.

Jamie Thom

Section 1: The start of compassion

A. Mental health in schools: it's time we talked
B. Aims and structure
C. The Crash
D. Picking up the pieces
E. Three for the price of one: understanding our hardware
F. What compassion is and what it isn't
G. How compassion-focused therapy addresses depression and anxiety and supports mental health

A. Mental health in schools: it's time we talked

In a recent interview, I heard an author say that you write a book to find out what you really think about something. Well, I agree.

It should be an exciting time to be a teacher: luminaries such as Hattie and Wiliam have rightly shifted discussion around education to a focus on what *actually* works rather than what we think or assume will work to support our students. But for many, 'exciting' isn't the word they'd use to describe their working lives. Obsessive measurability, hyper-accountability and the dire straits of recruitment are making workload and conditions intolerable. Alongside this, there has been a serious paucity of attempts to really help educators get to grips with uncertainties of the ever-changing educational landscape, let alone put them a position to help their students.

Mental health is something that we are rightly increasingly hearing lots about, not just in teaching but in wider society. It's not clear whether this is because we are sadder than we were previously, the world is harder to tolerate, or it's just more OK to talk about now. Sadly, though, increased publicity has left real understanding lagging miles behind. Glance at many schools' calendars and you'll find 'well-being days' dropped in – perhaps even half-termly for the more enlightened. Even then, well-being extends to a Wednesday afternoon off every six weeks if we're lucky.

I'm a bit of a geek, and in my favourite film of all time, *The Dark Knight Rises*, my favourite scene is when Commissioner Gordon lambasts his colleague for waiting for the army to come and save them from Bane detonating his nuclear bomb: 'This only gets fixed from *inside* the city!' Well, sorry, but Ofsted can't fix this. School leaders can, to a degree; but ultimately, it's down to *all of us* to play our part in making mental health a meaningful and workable part of education. In truth, given the rate of change we are experiencing in modern schools, the response in terms of helping school leaders, teachers and students to understand this has been no more than a drop in the ocean.

In the wonderful recent BBC Two documentary *School*, one colleague asserted that education does not really care about the *well-being* of young people. It does, I suppose, to the extent that grades improve life chances; but frankly, we're in fart-in-hurricane territory with that line of thinking. I don't think education *knows* how to care for people's well-being, so what does it do? It gropes around in the dark, clawing at tangible measures and indicators that demonstrate things are working. In actual fact, I would argue that focusing on data and outcomes comes at a greater expense than anyone could have possibly imagined. And whether we like it or not, if we want education to be successful, we have to look after the people in it.

And all the while, our approach to the things we are most at risk of in the current climate – anxiety and its best friend, depression – is at best naive and, in some cases, wilfully ignorant. We're happy to be told that depression is a chemical imbalance in the brain, and we're happy to see it as some kind of disease. The short-sighted medicalised view of depression is oversimplified, but I can understand where it comes from: you're less likely to be criticised if you've got something wrong with you genetically, or you've got something akin to a bacterial infection, I suppose. As well as this, we often internalise and blame ourselves for things we feel, because in some kind of weird way it helps us to make sense and take control of the difficulties we experience. So what exactly is my point? However much we may even *want* it to be, it's not our fault: our brains are wired to perceive the world in a way that helps us survive, but we've had very little time – in evolutionary or indeed cultural terms –

to come to terms with mental health as a species. We need to get to grips with this fact. However, our brain is *not* a physical island: there's tonnes of information from our environment that we need to make sense of in order to function in our world. Sadly, the 'information' we process in educational environments can be toxic for our well-being.

B. Aims and structure of this book

'Human beings have largely conquered nature, but they have still to conquer themselves.'

Richard Layard

Our society's destiny is inextricably linked to the education it provides its citizens, and it's time that mental health was given a platform alongside pedagogy in policy – not only to keep citizens safe but to prepare them for modern life. Just as cognitive science has given us the resources to inform our curriculum and classroom planning, long before that, it gave us the resources to provide educators with the tools to sustain mentally healthy lives whilst supporting their students to do the same. This book is an exploration – and an explanation – of why, if education is to achieve its goals, it needs to go back to its core purpose by placing compassion at the heart of everything we do. I promise: this will be effective for every reason imaginable.

As I will detail below, 2018 was a fairly bleak year for me personally. Compassion-focused therapy (CFT) was what picked me up from my dangerously low nadir. This book uses CFT as a platform to suggest a healthier, more meaningful approach to mental health for all educators. It will inevitably have elements of theory within it – which I hope will be useful and necessary – but as someone experiencing CFT as a patient rather than as a practitioner, I will use only the most pertinent theoretical aspects for the purposes of this book. I see no point in branding this as a particular approach to teaching; rather, having explored the basis of the theory, I want to then relate it to some of the wider contextual aspects of teaching at political, school and classroom level to help us better understand the lives we lead as educators. I am fortunate to have worked and collaborated with some truly exceptional practitioners in the classroom, so later on I'll explore some of the best time-saving yet impactful approaches to teaching that I've developed/adapted/stolen and that fit being a compassionate teacher – not only in terms of ourselves but our students.

The first part of the book is rather more explanatory in nature before the second half becomes more suggestive and constructive in terms of next steps. **Section 1** begins with a frank and honest disclosure of where this book came from: my own experiences. To be honest, the thought of putting this out there is a little more frightening now I know it is going to print. If any of it resonates with you, or you can relate to it in a way which is meaningful, then it's not been time wasted. It might not resonate, I suppose, but even if you can reflect on some of your own warning signals, then again, it's worthwhile. The section then moves on to exploring the basics of CFT (to get us going), including a clear and concise explanation of what is actually meant by 'compassion'. It includes interviews with CFT therapists to help explain the most important aspects of the model. Having defined the key elements of the model, **Section 2** moves on to exploring the inherently threatening context of modern education from government to classroom levels, and why compassion offers us a genuinely workable solution to the problems we face. Here, I am fortunate to have enlisted the support of some of the most credible people in education today – including Mary Myatt and Dame Alison Peacock – as well as formidable middle and senior leaders who speak candidly and from the heart when it comes to leading in the modern context. It also features Professor Jonathan Glazzard of Leeds Beckett University, who has undertaken impressive research around mental health within the teaching profession. **Section 3** explores how we can begin to reframe our professional lives using compassion. In effect, this section explores how compassion can transform the most important driving force in education: relationships. This includes the relationships we have with ourselves, as well as our colleagues and the students in our classrooms. It also introduces further aspects of CFT and offers tangible observations and advice to help us move forward. **Section 4** focuses on the more tangible suggestions for compassionate teaching and learning, especially in terms of reducing workload and ensuring best value and impact from the time we dedicate to our profession. **Section 5** offers some final thoughts and suggestions for reclaiming our profession, and **Section 6** offers some further reading, should you wish to pursue any aspects of the book in greater depth.

C. The Crash

'*Mum, I've just totally lost my place in the world.*'
Me

I'll start by being blunt: 2018 was the worst year of my life. When it began, I didn't know it would be the year that I would experience something so intensely miserable that it would push me to even consider taking my own life. Someone I went to school with took his own life a few years ago. I remember thinking: 'Why? What causes you to what to do that? It's so alien.' Well, I found out in 2018.

Work-related stress and anxiety pushed me into a depression that forced me to question everything I had ever known. This chapter, affectionately titled 'The Crash', is the summation of me limping from January through to April thinking I would be fine. I have always been an advocate of the place of mental health in education and wider society, and as an admittedly overly sensitive person (I teach English – it comes with the territory) I've never been far from anxiety and that type of thing. But what happened between Easter and – well, what is still happening to me – was nothing less than an education in the severest possible terms about what 'mental health problems' means.

It was the Easter holidays. I had been sat in the lounge with my parents, wife and little boy making plans for the coming months. When Mum asked if we needed her and Dad to look after our son – Wilfred – something shifted in my mind. I was intensely relieved that they'd offered to help us out on a weekend we were due to be away, but the relief somehow seemed drastically disproportionate. I was breathless, my heart palpitated, and my mouth was dry. I panicked, and I couldn't put my finger on why. Unbeknownst to me, what was brewing inside me was about to rear its head in a way far beyond anything I could anticipate.

I had been asked to step up as Head of English during a turbulent period at my school. It was an incredible amount of work, but also thrilling. I loved it: strutting my stuff and being able to formulate and execute all of what I thought were my ingenious plans that were going to change the world. At the time, I joked to a friend: 'Brogues, a Moleskine pad – I've arrived!' I was even told that I was 'holding my own' and being commended for my leadership. All good stuff. Easy.

My little boy had stopped sleeping a few months prior and I was running on empty, but powering through, working all hours and simply not stopping. I just assumed I could keep going back to the well. In my head, I was Harvey Specter from *Suits*. I even had a tie pin and a striped shirt with a white collar and a waistcoat. What was it Gordon Gekko said? 'Lunch is for wimps.' Well, sleep, fun, happiness and anything other than work was for wimps as far as I was concerned.

I lost sight of what connected me to the people around me at work: I'd always been someone who fought hard to protect my colleagues, but under massive strain I stopped fighting for my team. A couple of pretty unfair things happened and I should have stepped up and said something – but I felt powerless to stop my own negativity, let alone protect anyone else. I just went in on myself. My own fears began to manifest as seeing others as threatening. Seeing the worst in others is absolutely exhausting. If someone took time off, I would silently think, 'God, they've let me down. They're slacking.' My own misery was exacerbated because I totally lost faith in others' capacity for honesty and goodness. I was negative to my core, and so, it seemed, were other people.

My insides slowly accumulated pulsating, intolerable waves of guilt and shame. The situation was unscalable – so many insurmountable problems, yet so many probably solvable problems – but my brain could not distinguish between them. I felt blind.

On reflection – much to my bafflement now – I had ignored all the warning signs: checking my phone and waking in the night to add to my to-do list, working through lunch and dinner, not speaking with my wife and no exercise. I began to grow distant from my family as well: when Wilfred cried, that weight on my chest would increase; and when he came to hold my hand and ask me to play, waves of anxiety crushed my insides. I even ignored it when the wakefulness in the night became more frequent. However, that weight on my chest that started to characterise my mornings? It would surely just go away, I thought. This was life in the fast lane, wasn't it? How silly. In his masterpiece memoir, *The Noonday Demon*, Andrew Solomon captures the sneaking horrors of this with wonderful eloquence:

> The birth and death that constitute depression occur at once. I returned, not long ago, to a wood in which I played as a child and saw an oak, a hundred years dignified, in whose shade I used to play with my brother. In twenty years, a huge vine had attached itself to this confident tree and had nearly smothered it. It was hard to say where the tree left off and the vine began.[1]

Around that time, my brother – a person I have an unshaking love and respect for (I idolise him, truth be told) – jokingly commented that I'd 'died' on him. It hit me, to be honest; but I brushed it off. No time to waste.

Two months earlier at a family gathering, I remember remarking to Philippa – my wife – 'I feel like the Ghost of Christmas Past: no one gives a toss if I'm here or not.' I was angry, frustrated and upset, but I didn't really know why. That day, my mum had looked at me and asked, 'Where's my Andy gone? I've lost him.' I was a grey, tired, miserable shadow of myself, with huge bags under my eyes, lost under a pile of self-importance, work and stress. At the time, I recall the feeling inside me being somewhere between irritability and dismissiveness when I looked back at her; I was so, so angry. I thought she was being unsupportive and making it all about her when I was just being busy and successful.

---

1. Solomon, A. (2016) The noonday demon: an anatomy of depression. New York, NY: Vintage.

Anyway, back to my parents' house: I noticed a swathe of emotion overcome me and then leave me all at once; I didn't know what it was, but I just wanted to be alone. I took myself away to my parents' kitchen and sat there quietly. I felt unspeakably miserable. Beaten to the point of no return. Just utterly hopeless. Not only was I defeated, but now I realised the Harvey Specter suit I had been wearing was from Matalan, not Savile Row; I didn't have the finances, the corner office, or even a fraction of the success to go with it. I sat silently. I hoped to hell no one would find me, yet I was desperate for someone to come and pop their head around the door. I wasn't sure if I was supposed to be alone at that moment, or whether I needed someone to intervene. After about five minutes, Mum emerged and glanced at me. She asked casually: 'You alright?'

I looked up, held her in my eye for a second, and just shook my head. Then I burst into tears.

I was inconsolable. As I leaned into her, she cuddled me and said, 'Just struggling a bit, aren't you?' Somehow, that captured it. She got it. Maybe it was the recognition that I wasn't OK – just empathy and connection – but I felt safer. Still, I don't know what was more heartbreaking: conceding that things weren't OK; the thought of going back through to the lounge to tell everyone what an epic failure I was; the fact I couldn't be strong for my wife Philippa any more; or that my gorgeous little blue-eyed boy was running around without a care in the world, unable to comprehend the mess his dad was in.

However, my family were amazing. They had caught me: I fell backwards and had forgotten whether anyone really cared, but we resolved to work together to get through it. I drove home in tears, Philippa trying her best to console me.

It was all coming out now. That night, I rang my best friend, John, and told him I had taken one of those depression self-assessment tests on the NHS website, and had answered honestly that I felt it would be better if I wasn't here. Not-so-dormant parts of my mind began to consider planning the worst. It was then that I started to realise how serious things were. I was sobbing on the phone to him. Thank goodness he picked up.

In the coming months, I would be asked by various doctors if I intended to kill myself, and I would dismissively shake my head as if to say, 'Things aren't that bad.' But they were. I did go back to the psychotherapist I'd seen for a long time: she'd always helped. She had been amazing – but I sat there with her and just thought: 'Shit, this isn't helping. She was my trump card. I'm done now. This is really, really serious.'

I was in a fog, and I knew I needed to be looked after, so I headed back to my parents'. It wasn't fair to Philippa to ask her to watch me going through whatever this was, and it certainly wasn't fair to Wilfred either. Philippa's mum came down to help out for a few days – she was amazing. For those days, failing as a husband and as a father would just be two additional things I'd have to add to the list marked 'deal with later'.

When I – the prodigal mood-hoover and newly declared failure as I now saw myself – arrived at my parents' house again, I made my way up to a spare room in the house, found an old jumper of my dad's, and just lay on the bed squeezing it to my body. The next few days were somewhat of a blur. During the night I surfaced to use the bathroom, and my mum – who had obviously been awake all night worrying – found me, and asked 'You OK?' I just shook my head and we made our way downstairs. It was 3am. Pitch black. I lay on the couch and spoke in gasping breaths.

I'd left home some 13 years previously: I'd navigated university successfully, got married, had a child – heck, I'd even got a mortgage and held down a job, gaining steady promotions along the way. But there I was, reduced to a gasping, gibbering wreck. Back on my mother's lap, hoping she and my dad would pick up the pieces. They managed to secure me an emergency doctor's appointment. Without brushing my teeth or showering, and changing only into my jeans (but leaving my mucky hoody on), my mum led me by the hand into their doctor's and I sat staring wistfully into the distance, shivering. I'm known in my family for my extensive collection of hoodies. My brother even made me put on about ten of them while doing laps of the minibus on my stag do. But not even a hundred hoodies could have stopped me shivering at that point.

After my mum explained the situation to the doctor, I was prescribed sleeping tablets. The only crushing shame to me at that moment was that I couldn't take the tablet until bed time; I wanted to be knocked out. Not to experience what I was experiencing. (In the ensuing months I would be prescribed beta blockers, anti-depressants and diazepam.) I'm an avid Liverpool fan, and that night they were playing in the Champions League Semi Final. Usually, this would have been all I could think about. But I just sat there in front of the TV, waiting 'til 9pm when I could take my tablet. I even considered knocking back five or six. 'Bollocks to it,' I thought. 'I just need some respite.' I'm not daft: I'd read and heard numerous reports and accounts of mental health issues. But I could barely comprehend that this was now happening to me: all I could see was a mixture of sky blue and red colours moving around the screen. Literally. The opposition scored early; Liverpool were under threat. No reaction in me. Nothing. I just sat. Utterly apathetic.

I limped on. On the back of my new position at school, I went back to work despite my parents' concerned looks and the doctor's advice. Poor Philippa could barely engage with me whilst caring for Wilfred, who was passionately continuing his sleep strike. My parents would come before work to collect him to look after him; and on one occasion, I remember being dressed for work but just staring at my dad, desperate for him to say that they were taking me home with them. That the decision was being taken out of my hands. I wanted someone to do it for me, otherwise I'd be sacrificing my own career (as I felt at the time).

So I limped on, and went in. At the time, colleagues were commenting that I'd been losing weight: I dropped 30 pounds in four weeks. I remember speaking to my Deputy Head, lying and saying I'd had some 'troubles with circulation' over the holidays, but that I was now fine. Sounds ridiculous now (in fact, it did at the time as well, and we both knew it). I felt this was the safest option given that the permanent job offer of Head of Department sat in my pigeonhole downstairs in the staff room. She's not stupid; she's probably the most perceptive person I've ever known. She's got this knack of drawing answers out of you that you didn't know you already knew. She looked at me and she knew.

Truth be told, in those months I don't know how I functioned. I went into some kind of approximation of how I thought I should be performing in front of the students and my team. But it wasn't until Philippa directed me to a compassion-focused therapist that I could even begin to acquire the knowledge or perspective necessary for picking up the pieces of my life. The warmth and love of family is crucial, but equally crucial is the recognition that there are experts whose training and experience can help us understand ourselves as human beings. I wouldn't even say that this was when the pieces started to be picked up: the therapist I saw provided me with the tools to begin to see the pieces that could be picked up.

Philippa's role cannot be overstated, and before I reflect on the process of healing, I've asked her to give her side of the story. Mental health impacts on those around you. I know it took its toll on those closest to me, and I understand that.

. It was Jan 2019 just after a family trip away when Andy first floated the idea of writing something of my own in his book. At first I questioned the relevance and was keen that it wouldn't take anything away from the book and his experience. After a conversation that concluded with something like 'mental health doesn't just affect the individual: it's systemic and families feel it too', I agreed to share a brief insight into how I experienced this last year.

. Before I go on, some context. I am a clinical psychologist – Dr Sammons(!) – and I work in the NHS with people who are struggling with poor mental health in the most severe sense. I listen to people's narratives, their journeys and struggles every day at work. I work systemically with families and carers who support the people I see and who also need support themselves. You might therefore think I can offer some important insight into 'the crash' that Andy experienced. You may even critically question: 'She's qualified; why didn't she see it happening? Why wasn't she proactive in supporting him? In preventing it getting worse?' These questions are not far off what my own emotional mind repeated for months on end – along with a hopeless 'I just don't know what to do. I'm a rubbish wife and a poor psychologist.'

. The truth is, you can't psychologise (if that's even a word. Cut me some slack – remember, I'm not the English teacher here) someone close to you; I was in it too. I'm not saying you can't support in an abundance of ways – you definitely can (though I'm sure many have done a better job of it than me). I couldn't be 'professional me' at home. I wanted to be the lifejacket, the person in the boat handing Andy an oar to climb up or the lifeguard encouraging him to carry on swimming because the shore really wasn't that far away. But most of the time, I was floundering in the sea with him, struggling to breathe as he did. I unhelpfully found myself riding the same waves. So all I can offer is my perspective as a human being, struggling alongside my husband as a wife and a mother trying to keep life going.

. I didn't experience an overnight realisation of how hard things had become. It was a gradual process, a sort of chipping away at the quality in our family days together. I first noticed the distancing. As a couple, we appeared to talk less; and when we did talk, it was all very functional: what did we need to do to get through the day? Who was picking our son up and when? Who would do the shopping? Who would put our little boy to bed? Then I think I noticed a general unhappiness creep upon me. I attributed this to the lack of laughter between us and I noticed that Andy had stopped planning or initiating things.

. It felt like his work had taken over and everything else was a distant second. I began to resent it. I mean, I didn't even know the people and processes he talked about but I began to passionately dislike everything about it. It felt all-consuming. Andy always seemed to talk about work; he was always on his phone in the evening and weekends – checking emails and responding to queries. We talked endlessly about switching off, not doing work in the evenings, disconnecting school emails from his personal phone – that sort of thing. In the moment he would agree it was a good thing to do; but he was never quite able to put it into practice. Eventually, each time I mentioned it he would look at me with a sort of scared expression as if he was fearful of even the thought of 'switching off'. I wondered if it was just too much, too frightening to disconnect. I remember one evening saying to him something like 'You need to set boundaries for yourself. Others won't set them; and if you respond to emails late at night, this sets people's expectations up and they will continue to email.' He understood what I was saying – he really did – but the response I got was 'Teaching is different from psychology. If I don't reply, it makes my life harder in the long run.' I sighed, overrun with feelings of helplessness myself.

. Andy and I are a fairly modern couple. We both work full time and we both share equal parenting roles as well as looking after the house. Neither of us spends more time at home than the other, so the sharing of tasks just seems logical. However, this does mean that balance is crucial. For example, if I have a sickness bug, or our little boy isn't sleeping, everything gets thrown out of kilter. There wasn't – and still isn't – much room for error. Neither of us can easily drop the ball without it putting significant pressure on the other. When the depression showed up for Andy and took him away from the present, I felt a pressure. Everything in the house fell to me. Understandably so, given the turmoil and general disconnect that Andy was now experiencing. But it was exhausting; and to top it off, I didn't feel I was helping in any way, shape or form. Andy was caught up in a self-destructive narrative and continued to spiral further away from me. I remember thinking, with all this going on, 'I am a rubbish wife! I need to do better in order for things to get better.' Really compassionate, right? But it felt true: I felt like I was trying to do everything and doing a rubbish job of it.

On reflection, this last year has sent me through a rollercoaster of emotions – and I have said things that were definitely unhelpful at times. It wasn't until I burst into tears on a family day out that I realised I too was starting to struggle. We were walking round our local park one day – a park we both love. Andy was talking about the issues at school and the upset as a result of these issues. I remember we got to the cricket pitch, and as I looked out over the field, a tear rolled down my cheek and I realised I was really upset – and actually bloody angry. We had made the effort to go for a walk with our little boy to get fresh air and have a day out together and all I could think was: 'I need Andy to be quiet and leave me alone. I can't cope with him talking any more about how terrible school is. I can't listen any more.'

It was all too much when I thought this out loud. I know it's awful. So utterly the wrong thing to think – let alone say to someone who is struggling. But in that moment I was overwhelmed, kicking back and wanting to avoid the aversive narrative. My thoughts told me I was upset at him for ruining the efforts we had put into 'spending some quality time together' – and this made me angry because goodness knows we both needed it! Then it went wider: I was angry at the education system and the fact that it was happily – as I saw it – ruining families. It placed value on all the wrong things and that annoyed me. I was compelled to walk off. Where had my resilience gone? My compassion and understanding? The attributes I try so hard to maintain at work I was failing miserably with at home.

Framing this experience within a CFT model, my threat system was activated every time Andy shared with me the traumas in his working world because – heck – what he was talking about was now my world, too.

His pain had become mine. My soothe system was screaming 'You need space! You need to look after you!' The brief few minutes I had in the park by myself afforded me some clarity, and in that moment I cried. Underneath it all, I felt so lonely. Andy appeared to have changed so dramatically, and most of the time I just really missed him. In making room for the pain, I came to realise what I value the most: my husband, my family.

D. Picking up the pieces

'Compassion is the antitoxin of the soul: where there is compassion even the most poisonous impulses remain relatively harmless.'
Eric Hoffer

I have always been what you might call an anxious person, I suppose, and I understood the issues linked with worry and mental health. But such was my current mental state that I was petrified there was no way back. I recall staying with my brother around that time, and just looking up at him with a huge lump in my throat, barely managing to say: 'I think this is going to finish me, mate.' I was convinced it would.

I remember going to see my therapist for the first time. The chair wasn't very comfortable, and nor was the room I saw her in (we now meet at her other location, which has those springy wooden Ikea chairs – much more agreeable). She seemed nice, but not commanding. At the time, I felt I wanted someone to tell me what was up, and how to fix it, and I wasn't convinced. One thing she did say was that she was confident that I could be put back on the right track. That was nice. Something she showed me in that first meeting has remained with me since, and it has given an entirely different texture to the way I process the world. It was only when I got home and talked to Philippa about what we discussed that a vague dawning of understanding occurred.

As I recall, I would sit in my classroom, feel a tightness in my chest and just breathe heavily. Being utterly and entirely overwhelmed about my workload, I'd effectively have whole mornings experiencing panic episodes. This was my new-found success, though. I was trapped, with no way out. I wouldn't take my jacket off because I felt it was some kind of protective layer. I must have looked very strange in the middle of a hot summer walking around school with a tight-fitting Superdry jacket on. At this stage, the simplicity of the model suggested by my therapist helped me to separate from my own thoughts and do what psychologists call 'defusion'.

In a nutshell, we are not our thoughts. We might think we are, but we're not. If we can recognise a thought we are having, and spot ourselves having it, then it becomes less intense. They say a problem shared is a problem halved; well, I'd say a thought noticed is a thought de-intensified (not as catchy but I'll work on it). Of course, when you defuse something and spread it thinly, it becomes less intense; and when a problem becomes less intense, it becomes easier to think about solutions. In psychological terms, we should think more about 'defusion' – in other words to 'unfix' or 'loosen' the connection. When we fuse with our thoughts, we begin to see them as factual even though often we are merely conjecturing. Effectively, we need to create space between ourselves and difficult thoughts and feelings, or we can wrongly accept them as facts and become fused with them. Over time, this can impact how we feel and behave.

The genius of this model is that it can be understood by anyone, but it is in fact underpinned by the most elemental aspects of the human brain (so basically, it's sound). I'm going to introduce it here but go into more depth about the inner workings and its relevance to education below. Effectively, the brain has three parts that need to be in sync for us to be functioning healthily. At the moment, it's important to recognise that 'compassion' sits in the middle of these three circles. Only when these are truly in perspective can we be compassionate in a meaningful way – more on this later.

Emotional Regulation Systems

Paul Gilbert's evolutionary model proposes that human beings switch between three systems to manage their emotions.

Each system is associated with different brain regions and different brain chemistry.

Distress is caused by imbalance between the systems, often associated with under-development of the soothing system.

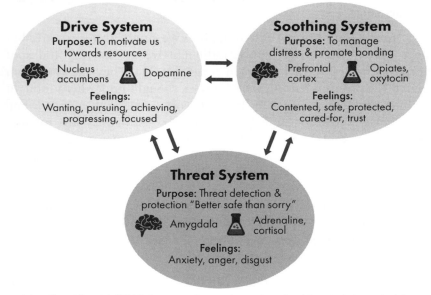

Adapted from: Gilbert, P. (ed)(2005). *Compassion: Conceptualisations, Research and Use in Psychotherapy*. Routledge.

Mindfulness & Clinical Psychology Solutions (2018) 'Your brain's 3 emotion regulation systems'. Available at: www.bit.ly/2IpsgLX (Accessed 4 Oct 2018).

The model showed me that the threat part of my brain was basically on fire; it had taken over and overridden my consciousness. Long-term anxiety had beaten my mind into such a state that I was used to feeling like a failure, and the pattern-seeking side of my brain would look for more opportunities to endorse my new-found worldview as a failure. I'd receive emails from people at work in the mornings – they would be sat waiting for me in my inbox (the inbox was on my phone, so accessible at night, too) and my head would explode, and I'd cry sitting at my desk. I'd *completely* lost the ability to credibly distinguish between 'threats'. Ironically, nothing had changed since the brogue comment; but at the same time, *everything* had changed, because my mind had developed a whole new lens for interpreting the world.

To illustrate this point, my brother is very successful financially. He drives a Range Rover Evoque (which he plays down, but I love it) and runs two successful businesses, one of which turns over in excess of £1.5m. Despite his protestations that his life is not perfect, at the time I would not believe him. I fixated on the fact that teaching would never pay me enough money. That I was an idiot for choosing this profession. That I was a mug. I entirely lost sight of the fact that I'd always loved and been almost smug about my profession. I also began to fixate on my university friends who had been 'brave' enough to work in London and, in my head, were now working in flashy high rises, relishing the pressures of high-paid jobs, and who would retire early and float around the Mediterranean on their yachts while I, a 70-year-old failure, would drag myself into work to be verbally abused by snotty kids. (Only now, with some regained sense of reality, can I remember once being stood in a classroom and laughing to myself, thinking 'Someone is actually *paying* me to do this! It's ridiculous! I love it!')

At the time, my brother came to stay with me when Philippa was away, and he said, 'I knew there was something up when you started asking me about franchise cleaning businesses. You weren't the person I respect more than anyone else and who can reach me in a way no one else can.' He doesn't know this, but I bit back a tear at that moment. I heard his words, but I had totally lost any sense that anyone could ever feel that way about me. I clearly remember looking up to my mum around that time and saying, tearfully, 'I've totally lost my place in the world.' We had a number of really nice things lined up at that stage at weekends – trips away to friends, tickets to the *Harry Potter* show in London, and visits to family in the Scottish Borders. All of this I found teeming with threat, sadness and hopelessness. Philippa was a tower of strength; goodness knows how she put up with me.

Anyway, it was never going to be an overnight fix, but the diagram that the therapist drew and laid on the table (and still lies on the table in our sessions now) at least gave me a first step into understanding what the hell was happening to me. Now, picking up the pieces meant recognising I was in 'threat mode'. As a still-vaguely sentient human being, I was able to talk about what were once my 'drives' and what I found 'soothing.' It gave me some kind of way in to access different parts of my brain and what had once been my happier states of being.

E. Three for the price of one: understanding our hardware

'Wisdom, compassion, and courage are the three universally recognized moral qualities of human beings.'
Confucius

You'll be pleased to know that this isn't an evolutionary psychology book (if this is, by some weird quirk, a disappointment, please read no further and return this book). Far superior and more knowledgeable academics than I have written with great wisdom on this topic. However, what follows is a very short rationalisation of the stuff which will help you get to grips with what CFT actually is. With this as the platform, we'll explore the significance of it in an educational context in the chapters that follow. I'll bring in other elements of the model where relevant, but we need the basics first.

Everything about the world we live in encourages us to compare (and define) ourselves in relation to things that are to varying degrees outside of our control: the success of others, material possessions, even relationships. Even the most fundamental elements of human experience are now mediated by human inventions: we can't really do anything without using something that is manmade. Fortune 500 companies dominate our economy and control our working patterns: post-industrial society is now our matrix. As humans, we are often socialised into knowing that things like compassion, honesty and kindness are good virtues to have, but our everyday existence seems to encourage another set of behaviours entirely if we are to be 'successful'.

An English teacher by trade, I often think about words. The 'ness' on the end of 'happiness' turns the adjective 'happy' into a noun (a thing). The danger here is that we come to view happiness as something that can be reached/grasped/purchased/bartered for. We've all heard things to the effect of happiness being about 'the journey, not the destination', but why do we so frequently forget this? I could give you a list of who I might call the happiest people I know, yet they are not united by a commonly held high status, wealth, health, set of achievements, exam results, or anything else. What unites them, then? I'd say something that lies at the cross-section of perspective and contentment – nothing more, nothing less. Meanwhile, I have a self-diagnosis of what I call the 'car syndrome' – if I see someone driving a nice car, my mind automatically (probably perversely) says 'I wish I was that person; they are definitely happy' and I fall into the old trap of judging someone else's outsides against my insides.

I keep doing it. And I'll probably never stop. The key is to make oneself aware of this in order to defuse and make the negative feelings less intense. It's not difficult to name examples of people in our lives that have struggled with mental health problems. What unites us *all*, however, is our biology – and more importantly for the purposes of this book, our *humanity*. Mental illness is widely accepted to be indiscriminate: it does not care about social standing, status or wealth, despite what we often unthinkingly assume.

We rightly marvel at the awe-inspiring wonder of the human brain. The CFT model recognises that around two million years ago, humanity's capacities of reasoning, reflecting, anticipating and imagining enabled us to race to the top of the food chain. However, when we are born, the instruction manual that doesn't come with our brains fails to mention that our minds can be as much a hindrance as they can a support in helping us make our way through life. In a nutshell, our brains are just as (if not more) likely to create problems as they are to solve them. In the incredible book *Sapiens*, Yuval Noah Harari makes the point that we can think six false things before we've even had our breakfast (I think he was underplaying it to be honest).

If we assume that evolution is truly a 'survival of the fittest'-type scenario, it seems odd that millions of years has resulted in such a fundamentally flawed piece of hardware for making our way through life. In fact, though, evolution is about adaptation, reproduction and thriving numerically, but only in the sense of *survival*: nowhere does evolution cater for mental health, which is perhaps why we are only now as a society moving anywhere near being able to understand it.

As humans, we have basic stuff we all want: sex, status, pleasure and attachment, and our emotions and feelings about the world make up our very own satnav system to guide us to fulfil these goals. Evolutionary psychology tells us that humans actually have three brains for the price of one. And as we evolved and thrived, we didn't really leave behind the most primal parts of the brain; we just evolved to do more complex stuff which enabled us to rule the roost. The result is that, as human beings, we need to make our way through life with a brain that isn't completely well adapted to solve problems encountered in 21st-century living. Our brain has three parts:

*2 million
years ago*
Soothe system:
neocortex
Evolved in primates and is
around two million years old.
It allows us to have abstract
thoughts and an imagination.

120 million years ago
Drive system: *mammalian*
Came about with mammals. It records memories and
experiences. The origins of status, hierarchy and pecking
orders are traced to around this stage.

500 million years ago
Threat system: *reptilian*
Controls the most basic stuff: heart rate, breathing, body temperature.

My (probably rather crude) understanding of the human brain is that is has three aspects. The most elemental part (the reptilian 'threat') system is designed to help us simply survive: fight, flight or freeze. We then have the mammalian system, which is linked with status, achievement and a sense that we are important (linked to memories and associations to help us understand where we are in the grander scheme of things, also known as 'drive'). Finally, we have the human-specific 'soothe' system, linked to attachment, connection and safeness. 'Soothe' is what operates when there is no competition for perceived resources and no threats to be dealt with. Sadly, for many, truly uncomplicated access to the soothe system is a difficult thing.

Let me work an example here. We might have noticed that our breathing is a bit heavy, and our heart rate is up to a slightly uncomfortable level (reptilian brain: check). Maybe we didn't get the job we wanted, or we're teaching that God-awful class in the morning, or someone at work is treating us like a pleb – thereby potentially triggering negative memories of other times, emotions or feelings when we have been treated as such (mammalian brain: check). However, just as we notice this, we also have a worry and a concern that we might be a failure in general too, and this can become bound up within the way we perceive ourselves intrinsically. Yes, this is an extreme example, but the ability to posit and create hypotheticals is not only our greatest strength, but also arguably our Achilles heel.

Mental health issues arise when these three systems conflict or misalign with one another in some way. If all we experience is failure, our threat system might eventually continually override what causes our 'drives' – and we lose hope and become depressed. We see this happening in other species too, by the way; depression, believe it or not, has an evolutionary basis.[2]

The crucial thing to remember is that the 'soothing' brain is where the answer lies: practising being kind and constructive to oneself – and not falling into the traps of shame and guilt – can profoundly change the way we see ourselves and the world. I will unpack this relationship – and how our education system is less than helpful in this respect, and what we can do about it – in later sections. In essence, though, it is a decent starting

---

2. Gilbert, P. (2006) 'Evolution and depression: issues and implications', *Psychological Medicine* 36 (3) pp. 287–297.

place to talk to ourselves as we would hope a friend would: with kindness and honesty (in other words, compassion). Humans are at the top of the food chain for a reason: they learned to cooperate. Just a thought.

At the time, though, 'kind' was the last thing I was being to myself: I remember beginning to feel ashamed that I was a teacher, that I hadn't gone into the city and made millions. My brain had plucked a deep insecurity from my mind and placed it front and centre for me to think about all day.

In the same way, though, it's not difficult to see how high-powered and highly successful individuals live life with 'drive' to avoid failure, being fuelled by threat – but the moment they experience failure, it is catastrophic for their mental health; and I would suggest that even if they don't experience failure, equally destructive burnout will eventually occur with a lack of soothe anyway. Later on, we will explore the finer details of this in the context of schools. In a nutshell, however, the neocortex is the key to our evolutionary sweet shop – every inch as much a curse as an opportunity. We just need to know how to understand it.

To be honest, in order to orient our way through the world, we need a certain amount of an 'inner critic' to understand how to gain resources and achieve. Looking at the potentially conflicting drivers and goals of these three systems, it is hardly surprising that mental health problems are something so many of us experience. So, because humans are fantastic at self-sabotage, it makes sense we're wired for mental health problems on an individual level too, I suppose.

Contrary to some people's beliefs, it's not about *removing* the reptilian brain; it's about *understanding* it and seeing it for what it is. Post-industrial society – which accounts for a miniscule fraction of our overall evolutionary timeline for something that shapes the experience of our existence – encourages us to forget that our brain's hardware evolved in response to an entirely different set of circumstances to the ones we face today. Note that this works on a societal level too – wars, conflicts, social tensions and racism all stem from what Harari calls our remarkable ability for 'fiction' (i.e. things which become fact because they are believed). Adolf Hitler sold his people one of the worst pieces of fiction in human history when you think about it. In terms of our survival, it seems counterintuitive to fight wars for countries that exist only on a map, and to sacrifice one's life in the most appalling ways – unless our threat system was being fuelled in a way that leaves us with (what we perceive to be) no other choice. Again, we'll explore this below in terms of the ecosystems of schools and how we might be able to reimagine this.

I'd imagine a reptilian brain was pretty damned handy when running from a lion or just making sure we – *ahem* – do the thing that ensures our genes are left behind. And I'm sure a mammalian brain was great for staying safe and respected amongst one's peers in a chaotic and dangerous world. Whilst these things are not a total irrelevance nowadays, let's face it: the complexity of these issues pales into insignificance compared to the kinds of problems we face in modern life. Unfortunately, the most powerful part of our brain is the bit which acts as the override in case of threat; and when you combine that with our new-found ability to create and conjecture, our brains are, at times, not so wonderful.

However, this is where CFT comes in: by being more understanding of ourselves, we gain a much greater sense of clarity about the suffering of others, too. Ultimately, CFT encourages us to look inwards – *honestly and courageously* – to understand and come to terms with the conflicting hardware in our heads. The antidote to the threatening world we live in lies in what Paul Gilbert calls 'prosocial behaviours': the idea of altruism and cooperation was our evolutionary queue-jump card, and it's also our modern antidote too.

CFT starts with the most fundamental truth we can know as humans: although we didn't choose to be here, and we didn't seek to be alive in any conscious way, what we can do is know that the most important relationship we have is with *ourselves*. Only when we truly understand our own hardware can we properly and meaningfully turn to people around us and say: 'Just like you, I'm here, I'm human, I didn't choose to be here. Let's recognise our common humanity.'

F. What compassion is and what it isn't

'*Compassion does not focus on the suffering that beings are undergoing, but on the beings undergoing that suffering.*'

Ogyen Dorje

It's easy to dismiss the idea of compassion: 'Oh, just be nice to yourself and others, then we can all sit around the campfire and sing Kumbaya.'

For the purposes of full disclosure, when I realised what the 'C' stood for, I was a bit downhearted. 'Compassion? I don't want to be told to be nice to myself; I like watching films and drinking cups of tea. I don't need to hear that it's OK not to get this or that done. It will just lead to more failure, and I don't want that!' To an extent, I was right. But what Philippa explained to me was that it takes more courage to be truly compassionate to yourself – and others – than I could possibly have fathomed at that stage. Compassion *does not* mean popping the kettle on and lying on the sofa. It might mean that *sometimes*, though (you might be glad to hear), and that's the point. The constant aspect in our minds that we are trying to develop is honesty, but not the brutal, uncompromising kind; it's the kind of honesty that is framed with warmth and understanding. When times feel tough, we're not saying, 'Don't be stupid, stop being pathetic and get on!' We're saying, 'There's a reason I'm feeling this way. It might feel difficult, but I understand why I need to move forward, and I will do so by noticing and recognising these feelings. And I'm doing this because it's in my best interests.'

Picking the word apart, the Latin root 'com' means 'with' and 'passion' ironically initially came from the Latin word 'pati' meaning 'to suffer' (think about the idea of *The Passion of the Christ*, for example), rather than the intensely loving yearning we link with the word today. (Although the 'suffer' bit seems oddly apt for present purposes.) When you are moved to act by some kind of external force in spite of the suffering, this is the true notion of 'passion'. Now for Gilbert's definition of compassion, which is:

> 'a sensitivity to suffering in self and others with a commitment to try to alleviate and prevent it.'

For me, compassion is about honesty and warmth. Allowing ourselves to recognise what is good for us is *everything*: sometimes, curling up on the couch, watching a film and ordering a takeaway might be just what is needed to give us some time to decompress (you've probably spotted a common theme here: yes, I love my couch). However, compassion is *not* about becoming what my dad would call a 'slovenly git' and not recognising our need for exercise, healthy food, and spending time with others, for example. Compassion and self-care are about recognising that our needs (and those of others) are fluid and transient.

It's OK to push oneself to do more, to want more and to be outside of our comfort zones, as long as it's in line with our core values. Remember that there's a difference between compassion and *sympathy*: with sympathy, you have a gut emotional reaction to a person or a situation – it's emotive; whereas compassion is inherently more considered. Nor is compassion the same as *pity*: I can't imagine anything productive coming from constant self-pity and resignation. The key difference is the compassionate voice that we need to develop with ourselves, rather than the critical, shaming voice that so often drives our decisions and the way we see the world.

So, with compassion, there is an honest warmth to what we're doing. It's hard, and it takes time (I'm still not there myself). Some days, fear and anxiety find me more easily than others; but the difference now is my perspective on them. But as with all things psychological, it's not about an end state; it's about the *intent*. Each time you *notice* the subjectivity of your thoughts, think of it like a minute on the treadmill or one repetition of a weight at the gym – it's strengthening our ability to climb out of our self-imposed quagmires.

This model recognises that the human brain – the 2-million-year-old one – is extraordinary in its potential (have a read of *Sapiens* if you want to know just how much we've paid for a brain the size we have). The good news is that what moved us to the top of the food chain is our ability to cooperate and be altruistic. This, ladies and gents, is where we find the answer to the evolutionary conundrum of three-brains-in-one. Warmth, honesty, attention and care are all fundamental to what got us here; we've just forgotten their importance in the pursuit of certainty through materialism, outcomes and measurability – all of which have taken root and become central to the way we perceive the world.

There is no doubt that the implications of this are immense for teachers and their students. What does this mean for behaviour management? What might this mean for workload and sustainability? How the hell can we take all this into account with a bunch of uncooperative teenagers in front of us? It takes real courage and energy to be sensitive to – and not simply dismiss – the suffering and experience of others. It's more than simply being sympathetic – and as you will know, humans can spot insincerity a mile away. Extrapolate compassion out to the hundreds of people you might encounter and even teach in a day, and this is mind-boggling. This, for me, is where the notion of commitment comes into play. I wouldn't suggest that we can just flick a compassionate switch and the world is all sunshine and rainbows. But I would suggest that a *commitment* to being empathetic and understanding is equally – if not *more* – important in our present context. Showing humanity, fallibility and genuine empathy reminds others of our common humanity, and it will encourage the realignment of our misaligned minds.

We've all seen the adverts, the marketing bumf, and we've probably all been told that rewarding relationships between teachers and their students are the heart of education. Some of us have probably even been on behaviour management courses or sat through long – dare I say tedious – behaviour management continuing professional development sessions designed to help us 'optimise our learning environments' (in fact, I'll check if that's been patented). What no one mentions is the period 6 Friday lessons with 10D3 after triple (insert subject here) when the students are either high as kites, lethargic, or just ready to switch off for the weekend and don't want to engage with whatever you have lovingly prepared for them. Nor does anyone mention the student that every now and then will totally throw you off your stride, the class that doesn't quite 'click' with you, or the infinite number of other possibilities that a school day might throw at you. We'll explore the practical implications of this in the classroom in later chapters, but I want to make the argument that with compassion at the heart of everything we do, schools will be a lot less threatening – and a lot more successful.

Here would be a good place to bring in the thoughts of two cognitive behaviour therapists who practise CFT. Together, Tracey Patrick and Clare Beavan operate MoodWise Ltd, a cognitive behavioural therapy (CBT) service in North Yorkshire. Given that my thoughts on this are not the thoughts of a professional, it's useful to have their perspective here before moving on to reflect on how CFT can address depression and anxiety.

What is the difference between CFT and mindfulness?

Tracey: Mindfulness is part of CFT and is used to help us bring our attention into the present moment. That can be a hard thing to do when our minds are used to being on automatic pilot for most of the time. So, if you are sitting in a staff room thinking 'I'm going to panic/be sick,' we can use mindfulness to notice our thoughts, emotions and physical sensations, enabling us to respond to the situation rather than react to it. Mindfulness is great for slowing things down, for connecting to ourselves, which in turn is great for activating our soothing system. Mindfulness helps you get into the 'here and now'.

Clare: Yes, I think it's a privileged position to be in for anyone to know how to notice shifts and changes. I think that mindful awareness helps with that – to say/notice 'Oh there's a knot in my stomach Where's that coming from? What's causing that?' – but it takes real strength too. Mindfulness techniques are used to influence and help the process of compassion-focused work.

As practitioners of the model, what is distinct about the approach?

Tracey: For me it's about the emotional shift that folk can make. In CBT we often use thought records to help work out what we are thinking. People are generally quite good at working out what they are thinking and often they can come up with alternative perspectives. So, they might decide 'I know I'm not a bad parent or a bad friend' but they won't really believe it. In therapy terms we call this a head-heart divide. CFT helps bring the head and the heart together – by exploring and practising how our posture, tone of voice and words impact on us. It helps us to connect to ourselves in a very powerful way.

Clare: Yes, you might do thought records, which are a useful CBT tool to use with people; but the problem is that sometimes, despite the evidence being there, people don't really trust the facts alone. As a therapist, it can feel that you're just (metaphorically!) twisting the person's arm into agreeing with the evidence (that's normally true) whilst the person is not feeling it. Sometimes it wasn't surprising if people came back for further sessions, because we hadn't really got to the head-heart level, where it begins to feel more genuine.

What makes CFT useful for people in particularly stressful jobs?

Clare: If I were to pick out professions that come frequently, I would say teachers, people in the banking sector, people in IT, and – believe it or not – quantity surveyors are my clients' four biggest areas. I noticed that the people who come specifically with stress seem to also find it useful in the way of viewing the organisation for which they work. People that have embraced CFT have often felt inspired to go back to the workplace and say, 'I'd like to be the mental health ambassador and I'd like to start introducing ideas into the workplace.'

Tracey: I would say I generally always have at least one teacher on my caseload.

I tend to explain emotional regulation very early on by drawing out the 'three circles' and I have never had someone say, 'That doesn't apply to me!' People quickly recognise what activates their threat system and can see that if their drive system is over-focused on achievement then that will just keep their threat system active.

People are often very surprised how underdeveloped/underused their soothing system is. Exploring how to activate the soothing system means we can take the heat out of the threat and drive systems – it gives us time to pause and slow down, to connect with ourselves and others and then help ourselves do 'the difficult thing' we're faced with.

CFT has wonderful potential to help us educate ourselves around our mental health, and people quickly start identifying which system is being activated and why. This is useful for all of us.

Is there anything in particular you notice about teachers?

Clare: I'm seeing one client, and we've been talking about breathing exercises and working to do some bits of grounding – but the biggest drawback is that there's physically no space in schools for teachers to practise these exercises, which I think is a real shame. We eventually had to resort to her thinking about sitting in her car to access that space.

Tracey: Teachers are so important and do a tremendous job in an ever-changing, target-driven political landscape. I'm the mum of a teacher – the *hours*, the *planning* and the *prep* are enormous. They work long hours and the job sets high expectations. If I was a teacher, my threat system would be permanently switched on. There is quite a bit of work being done to get compassion into organisations and Mary Welford is developing CFT work within schools.

G. How compassion-focused therapy addresses depression and anxiety and supports mental health

I also spoke with Dr Chris Irons, who is a leading proponent of CFT in the UK. His words about the model would be a useful place to begin this section:

Chris: CFT is a purposefully integrated psychological approach, drawing from multiple branches of science: from evolutionary ideas, from understanding of neurophysiology and neuroscience, attachment theory, social psychology and so forth. It essentially integrates ideas from many different sciences together, so it has overlaps with other approaches too because that's as it should be. What we've been striving for is a multimodal approach: rather than seeing that we can affect change just in one area or domain, there are multiple ways 'in' with clients. We can work with people and how they act and how they behave; we can work with their attention and what that's focused on, recognising where their minds are and where it would be more helpful to spend our time. Essentially, it allows us to say that if we struggle to bring change in one domain, we can work in another domain.

Gilbert asks whether we would, given the choice, live in a world with infinite resources and access to all the material things we'd ever need – but in return, we'd need to forego any human interaction. It's the same thing as the famous 'brain in a vat' scenario in which a mad scientist could remove your brain, place it in a jar and plug it into his magic equipment to simulate real life – and you would live the perfect life, by the way – would you do it? Most people say no. My wife probably thinks I would say yes, but I wouldn't – I promise!

Why? Because despite the world we live in, despite everything, we value relationships. It's hardwired into us.

Basically, the threat-detection system in our brain functions like a fire alarm: fantastic for getting people safe at the appropriate time; not so good at managing and navigating the subtleties of post-industrial human living. Imagine, then, if this fire alarm was going off all day, every day. True, you'd never be in the building and have no chance of being caught in a fire; but you'd probably be bloody cold and your other needs can't be met if you're stood outside waiting for the alarm to stop ringing. If your threat system is ringing and you are searching for potential threats, it's exhausting, and this has long-term physiological neurochemical effects. This is where I got to in April 2018, and, on reflection, it's what led to me wanting to no longer be here.

As the threat system overrides everything else, our ability to think reflectively and creatively is lessened: you can't reasonably expect to think of a way of explaining Pythagoras' Theorem to an 11-year-old if you happen to be running from a tiger at that moment in time. Long-term mistreatment in animals leads to retreatism and depressive behaviours. In other words, they adapt to being in what they perceive to be a threatening environment by adjusting their behaviour patterns. And it's the same with humans. Think about how stress can diminish our ability as humans to engage with – and educate – our students. Also, a young person from perhaps a violent or emotionally invalidating environment is not able to look for multiple explanations for their context: they invariably blame themselves. They associate relationships and the wider world with predominantly threatening scenarios, and this can go some way to explaining the experience and behaviours of the young people in front of us. Unsurprisingly, bellowing at a class only works a small fraction of the time. It's probably water off a duck's back to some students, while for others it does little more than trigger threat detection and shuts down any more meaningful cognitive processes. More of this later.

Looking at this from an evolutionary standpoint, if we are not threatened, then the right elements of creativity and intellectual curiosity can thrive. Modern educationalists have labelled this 'high challenge, low threat'. This is something for us to reflect on, not only as individual practitioners but at whole-school and human levels as well. In other words, through either implicitly or explicitly helping us to understand and empathise with ourselves and others, CFT is immensely powerful as it can help us to calm these threat protection systems with honesty, warmth and understanding. We can't avoid or escape our own minds, but we can *understand* them, and begin to nurture the most human part of ourselves.

In a nutshell, we need to be the change we want to see in the world. So, with all this bad news about our brains, there is some good news: we can do something about it. We *can* notice, and we *can* bring our 'soothing' systems back online. Think of it as a kind of physiotherapy for the mind (again, see Gilbert). In the short term (and indeed on an ongoing basis) we can do things like soothing rhythm breathing – plenty of guided videos of which you can find for free online – which actually activate mechanisms in the brain to calm us; and in the longer term, with heightened awareness and reflection, we can begin to step outside our thoughts, empowering ourselves to deal with the nonsense we are often surrounded with.

I don't really think this is possible without understanding our wider and personal contexts – which is what this book will aim to do, before offering strategies and considerations to walk the walk!

Key points:

- Our brain is the product of millions of years of evolution, resulting in three systems that regulate our emotions.
- These are the 'threat', 'drive' and 'soothe' systems.

- Mental health issues arise when these three systems become disproportionately aligned. In particular, overstimulation of the threat system can override our other systems, resulting in anxiety and depression.
- The compassion-focused therapy model relies on reflecting on these three systems to help us understand ourselves.
- In acknowledging these three systems, compassion-focused therapy draws on multiple disciplines, such as evolutionary psychology, cognitive behavioural therapy and mindfulness.
- We all share a common humanity, and it is crucial to recognise this in order to understand and alleviate suffering in ourselves and others.
- The key to gaining perspective is to develop our compassionate voice, which will allow us to view ourselves and others with honesty, warmth and understanding.

Section 2: Our threat-based context

A. Academisation and outcome-driven culture
B. School leadership
C. A teacher's life

> *'Only education gives us the power to go further.'*
> **Professor Becky Allen and Sam Sims**

When we reflect on the situation as it is, and the situation we ought to be striving for in schools, there is a huge disconnect. Professor Becky Allen and Sam Sims have written about this superbly in their book *The Teacher Gap*. Having read the book myself, one thing seems clear: we have got ourselves into a massive pickle, and we can no longer tell our backsides from our elbows. What follows is a reflection on the threat at every level of our education system, and the psychological implications. Mental health issues are a result of the individual and their environments, and these are, of course, profoundly interrelated. There is a sense that, taking these two together at every level – from the wider system to the level of the individual – we need to ask whether the system is actually (albeit inadvertently) promoting poor mental health. Given that education is the most human of endeavours, this seems more than a little perverse. I'll start at the very top, and work my way down to the ground level.

A. Academisation and outcome-driven culture

When one looks into the history of academisation in England, and compares it to what currently lays before us, it's hard not to be reminded of *Animal Farm*, when Old Major's utopian vision comes full circle: 'The creatures outside looked from pig to man, and from man to pig, and from pig to man again; but already it was impossible to say which was which.' This is not to mention – *ahem* – the 'some animals are more equal than others' quote, as well. I don't necessarily mean that the utopia has descended into something horrendous; rather that the original purpose of academies has come to mean something else entirely than what was initially intended. In other words, to some degree we're here by accident. At the very least, there is a worrying disconnect between those running schools in this country and the stakeholders (caused by miscommunication – if we are being kind – or perhaps even wilful ignorance).

Compared with the departing Labour government's 1% of all schools in 2010, it was the incoming Michael Gove who put the programme on steroids, increasing academisation to around 60% of all secondary schools, and 20% of primary schools. Academisation was initially intended as a way of taking schools that were not doing the students justice out of local authority control. Irrespective of ideology or politics, it's possible to understand the rationale. Academies have more autonomy over how they spend their money and what kind of curriculum they offer. They have more freedom to do as they please to cater for their students, as well as their staffing structure. In small clusters – perhaps geographically – schools are also free to direct, structure and staff their schools according to need, sharing expertise where the need is most prevalent. There are, inevitably, winners and losers. Colin Harris has written insightfully about 'zombie schools',[3] detailing the plight of some schools (consisting of around 40,000 students) waiting to be taken over by multi-academy trusts (henceforth MATs). Based on the outcomes model, MAT leaders will be forced to evaluate whether taking on a school is in their best interests if their organisation is not to suffer. Again, this is not a rejection of academisation, but an acknowledgement that the context is altogether more complex than the solution proposed to solve it. (Don't even get me started on grammar schools.)

It's reductionist to dismiss our education system as placing outcomes – and not student welfare – at the heart of education. We need to examine this idea, and understand where it came from, and why it emerged. I'd like to make something very clear at this point: although I recognise the shortcomings of academies and free schools, I am not vehemently ideologically opposed to them. Rather, the risks that may go hand in hand with such a system of autonomy are concerning. Alongside the decreasing influence of unions, we don't really have any natural checks that promote well-being, because there is nothing in the system to meaningfully pay attention to it. In other words, if it isn't judged (or can't be judged), people tend not to worry about it. And saying that Ofsted is there to promote well-being is, well, misguided.

What the current structure does, though, is place well-being *entirely* in the hands of school leadership, which is at best unfair and – in some cases – dangerous. So, what happens in schools with the wrong types of leader? Well, in psychological terms, individuals with higher interest in 'social dominance' are not only less caring, but actively *exploitative*

---

3. Harris, C. (2018) 'Far too many children are victims of academisation', *TES* [Online]. Available at: www.tes.com/news/far-too-many-children-are-victims-academisation (Accessed 5 Oct 2018).

of others.[4] While some may feel they are a force for good, this cannot excuse inhumanity.

Although there are undoubtedly academies and free schools that do phenomenal work for the young people in their communities (one of which I am privileged to have worked for), whether that is a result of the system per se is another question. At the same time, I'm not entirely certain that we should look back at wholesale local authority control as a golden age for education in England; it brought with it a different set of issues. Many approaches in mental health are united in their focus on defusing and dissociating thoughts/narratives and facts. I hope this chapter goes at least some way to explain the context of modern education, at least through the eyes of a teacher.

In truth, a laissez-faire approach from the government has given license for some remarkable and inspiring practice in some places; but in others, it's created a vacuum for unscrupulous behaviour. What was intended as an invitation to freedom and diversity has in some cases led to the narrowing of curriculum offer and approaches. We must confront this, especially considering that academisation is not an automatic guarantee of success. In their recent report, the Education Policy Institute's executive findings state:

> Our principal finding through this extensive study is that academies do not provide an automatic solution to school improvement. As we demonstrate throughout this report, there is significant variation in performance at both different types of academies and Multi-Academy Trusts.[5]

So, surprise surprise, just as there was variability with the quality of local authority running of schools, there is variability in the quality

---

4. Niemi, L. and Young, L. (2013) 'Caring across boundaries versus keeping boundaries intact: links between moral values and interpersonal orientations', *PLOS ONE.* 8 (12).

5. Andrews, J., Perera, N., Eyles, A., Sahlgren, G. H., Machin, S., Sandi, M. and Silva, O. (2017) *The impact of academies on educational outcomes.* The Education Policy Institute. Available at: epi.org.uk/publications-and-research/impact-academies-educational-outcomes/ (Accessed 5 Oct 2018).

of MATs. However, the proliferation of what we might call a 'private sector mentality' brings with it its own set of issues. Yes, the present system allows for swifter interventions and so forth, but at what cost? I love a film quote, and am reminded of Dr Malcolm's words to John Hammond in *Jurassic Park*: on the subject of dinosaur cloning (make what you will of the metaphor), Malcolm says, 'Your scientists were so preoccupied with whether or not they *could*, they didn't stop to think if they *should*.' Barring ideological motivation, there can be little other reason to continue rolling academies out nationwide without due care and attention (thank goodness the government climbed down from this).

Alongside this, we now have the Progress 8 measure (designed to tell us how schools are doing with their students relative to their starting point at the age of 11 through to 16), which ranks schools in league tables locally and nationally. Schools whose students make progress are rewarded and graded positively; school leaders with the best grades are patted on the back; teachers whose classes do the best are rewarded with higher pay (or simply pay progression). Competition keeps us on alert and brings out the best in people. All fair, surely? And all in the name of ensuring the best education for students irrespective of their background and social status. Sadly not. Life on the 'threat/drive' axis works only for a short time: until either failure, burnout or both. This is happening at every level.

The shortcomings of this model are both moral and logistical in nature. At a fairly basic level, let's have a think about the language used by our inspection framework: encouraging any kind of growth mindset or risk-taking is almost impossible against this backdrop. 'Inadequate.' What a term. 'Requires improvement.' Lovely. What is that telling the staff of those schools? What is it telling the students and community? It's a national disgrace, to be frank. You can still have the same inspection outcome in terms of areas for improvement and development without such reductive labels.

A focus on the facts seems fair and objective, but what this ignores is that students of all abilities will not necessarily make progress at the same rate,[6] that – in spite of anything we do in school – *life* happens between Years 7 and 11. One thing I know for sure: saying 'we have no other way of measuring it' is a cop out, and it reeks of a lack of academic and moral integrity. Thus, teachers are being judged against classes that have had three or four years of education prior to the year or two they spend with teachers in an exam class. The students may well, by the time they reach their teacher, be well behind their trajectory as initially set out when they entered the school at the age of 11. Outcomes - unless communicated with purpose and integrity – will simply not speak to drive systems in any kind of meaningful way. Becky Allen's thoughts on Key Stage 2 driven targets help us to reflect on the moral dimension for students, too:

> [Students] who, for whatever reasons (chance, tutoring, high quality primary school, etc.) get high Key Stage 2 scores are then more entitled to support than those who have identical attainment now, but who once held lower Key Stage 2 scores. It would seem to be entrenching pre-existing inequalities in attainment. For me, the only justification for this kind of behaviour is some sort of genetic determinism, where their SATs scores are treated as a proxy for IQ and we should make no special efforts to help students break free of the pre-determined flightpaths we've set up for them.[7]

Map this onto the CFT model for a second: what attracted teachers into the profession – and indeed their drive for their work – is being overwhelmed by external threat factors quite outside of their control. It's horrible to think what this kind of narrative must be doing to young people as well. Students must have targets on the front of books and must be able to articulate their current grade and their target grade at all times to ensure they are always moving forwards.

This is not entirely the fault of school leaders – my goodness, must they feel the strain of these objective measures of their ability to perform

6. Killian, S. (2017) 'Hattie's 2017 updated list of factors influencing student achievement', *EvidenceBasedTeaching.org.au*. Available at: www.bit.ly/2T6tHmw (Accessed Oct 4 2018).
7. Allen, B. (2018) 'Poor attainment data often comes too late!', *Becky Allen* [Blog]. Available at: www.rebeccaallen.co.uk/2018/12/01/poor-attainment-data-often-comes-too-late (Accessed Dec 3 2018).

their jobs! Again, the misleading transparency of results, comparisons, league tables, Progress and Attainment measures forces a focus on the *outcomes*, often at the expense of the process. As we will see below, what then manifests is a focus on a range of tangible, measurable – let's face it – often *poor* indicators of learning. (Interestingly, the word 'education' takes its roots from the Latin 'educare' meaning 'to mould'; it takes time and a focus on the process to mould a shape out of something malleable.) No, I'm not proposing we forget outcomes, build a campfire and stuff daisies behind our ears whilst singing hand in hand; I'm just calling attention to the perversity of the situation we find ourselves in.

Ultimately, compassion is a long-term goal, and links with intrinsic motivation. Intrinsic motivation is intertwined with feeling that we have value, autonomy and purpose. Compassion is not something that lends itself entirely to short-term, extrinsic and tangible goals. By 'extrinsic', I mean a sole focus on things which are easily measured, and the 'if you can't measure it, it doesn't exist' mentality. One short-term measure, though, is about awareness: we need to start the conversation.

Georgia Holleran is a management consultant and pioneer of #teachwellfest. She offered some interesting thoughts into the present situation. Her views on the present culture we are faced with are both insightful and hopeful.

What's your link to mental health and education?

Georgia: I've been in education for 25 plus years now – and in management consultancy as well. Having come back and forth between those two worlds, I've realised there is nothing being done to look after the well-being of teachers. They are falling by the wayside just as much as anyone working in any corporation or any company I've been dealing with. I started *Teacher's Mental Health and Wellness*[8] in the hope of bringing some tangible stuff together. About a year later I had the idea of #TeachWellFest and I put together the festival within two months – and it's on the cards to run again this year.

---

8. www.teachersmentalhealthandwellness.com

Do you think there's something about the present context that is particularly concerning for you? Is it something that just has always been there and never gone away or is it something acute that's going on at the moment?

Georgia: Between the curriculum and Ofsted measures it's all got out of hand and it appears as if teachers are too busy or too exhausted to be militant and demand changes. More recently, I've noticed the increase in 'stuff to do' in schools too, and that's a big eye opener – even in schools where headteachers are well aware of the needs of their staff.

The current state of education – and of teachers in general – is something to do with the squeeze that's going on from all angles: from the government, from headteachers, from parents and from teachers setting impossibly high standards for themselves. However, looking at this in perspective, I think we're on a cycle. Something has to give and I'm wondering whether this gradual snowballing of teachers' mental health and kids' mental health is the start.

Do you think schools are in a position to do something about recruitment and mental health issues?

Georgia: I think *some* are. I'll qualify that by saying that a school with a good reputation will attract a lot of candidates, so there's more margin for error in those situations. It's all about the culture at the top and how that headteacher promotes and develops a positive working environment. What I'm seeing is some schools presenting a proactive online presence: they are getting onto Twitter and being a lively, attractive well-being driven school. Teaching doesn't mean you have to be back in the 19th century anymore. Teaching is a modern and engaging introduction to the world for our kids. But some schools are working so hard just to stay afloat or have agendas at odds with this idea.

So schools aren't necessarily powerless in this?

Georgia: No school is *powerless*. I think we will eventually get more headteachers who run terrific, wonderful, all-encompassing growth schools, and they will get recognised and commended by Ofsted. Until then, I suppose those headteachers will be working undercover and under great pressure if they don't get it right. There's nothing to stop headteachers doing more to protect their staff from the higher-level pressures a school has to bear, but they will have the sole responsibility if anything goes wrong. I'm sure some feel that in order to be new, creative, different and bold, you are also taking the risk of putting your job on the line.

Do you put this down to being outcome-driven?

Teachers don't seem to have an *identity* at the moment. It's affecting every workplace. One thing in education is that schools have to *compete*. They might not want to but they're jolly happy if they're at the top half of the table. We need to think about what we're saying to ourselves as well – the kinds of things we are saying to ourselves individually and on a school level. I suspect that in the heart of every tyrannical headteacher there was once someone who very much wanted to encourage others to learn. Somewhere along the line maybe that sense of competition has stoked the fire or awakened something else. What I'd call for is for people to be *aware* of themselves and *responsible* for themselves. As teachers we need to take a stand for ourselves; we can't wait for the government to do it. If we just start by making a stand for ourselves, and help others do it for themselves, then that trickle of a movement could turn into something bigger.

I was struck by Georgia's ideas around competition and a lack of identity in the profession. There is no doubt in my mind that the contextual strains are creating a fundamental lack of identity – not only for teachers, but for the profession as a whole. Simon Sinek talks about the 'why' and the thing that makes a company like Apple stand out from its competitors.[9] He says that it's simply because they know their 'why' and they communicate this much more effectively than their competitors. Rather than saying, 'Our product has X or Y – you should buy it!', they say, 'Everything we do challenges the status quo; we just happen to make great technological products. Wanna buy one?' It's because they have a core reason for being, and all stakeholders understand and are able to engage with it. Collectively, as an organisation, their drive is clear, based on innovation and redefining the status quo.

9. FORA.tv (2010) *The golden circle: why does Apple command loyalty?* [Video]. Available at: www.bit.ly/2Eiq8kU (Accessed 4 Oct 2018).

By contrast, I'm not entirely sure that education entirely understands its raison d'être any more. What is education actually for?

Fortunately, the CFT model operates at a macro level, too. Effectively, our profession has become disproportionately aligned and driven by threat and avoidance of failure. Not only does this lessen our ability to define and 'live out' the truly driving principles of education (whatever these may be), but the high stakes culture in which we currently reside has inevitable consequences – for present teachers, for those training in such a culture and for the young people in our classrooms. We're so bothered thinking about the 'what' of outcomes (after all, outcomes mean better life chances, right?), and dealing with the potential threats of not meeting those outcomes, that they have begun to define us and move us away from our core identity – the identity that attracted us to the profession in the first place. It keeps us busy, I suppose. But it doesn't make us smart.

I don't for a second think it's the fault of anyone or anything in particular, but we do have a responsibility to recognise the cycle we are caught in. Just as concerning is the notion that 'high threat' also lessens our ability to soothe and build those meaningful relationships that are supposed to be at the heart of education. I was fortunate enough to be an NQT at a wonderful school that took immense pleasure in sustaining its teaching and learning culture, and that encouraged and fostered a love of learning in trainees and new recruits. I feel genuinely sorry for those training in many contexts now, and I wonder how they can possibly grow and love their chosen profession.

At the time of writing, Amanda Spielman has made some rather promising comments about the ways that Ofsted are going to judge schools:

> For a long time, our inspections have looked hardest at outcomes, placing too much weight on test and exam results when we consider the overall effectiveness of schools. ... The bottom line is that we must make sure that we, as an inspectorate, complement rather than intensify performance data, because our curriculum research and a

vast amount of sector feedback have told us that a focus on performance data is coming at the expense of what is taught in schools.[10]

Before Ofsted or any governing body elects to act on this in a meaningful way, we must find a method of demonstrating and having intelligent conversations in schools about performance, and I'm not sure whether this can happen unless we begin to provide a wider educational experience that actually meets *all* students' needs. I'd argue that we don't have a clear enough understanding of what education is for (a la Sinek) in the first place; so instead, education measures its worth through data and performance in the name of equality and liberalism. But it's ended up being something that we simply did not intend it to be in the first place.

Linked to this, I remember a question-and-answer forum I attended some years ago. The links to *Animal Farm* are yours to make. Dominic Cummings (then the advisor to Education Secretary Michael Gove) answered questions from classroom teachers about the future of education. I remember being compelled and in agreement with what he said about freedom from the state, freedom to deliver curriculum offer to students, and freedom to spend money where schools see fit. This was all in the service of transparency, honesty and outcomes. Now, I wonder whether 'freedom' is slightly misleading given the central focus of data and outcomes in order to judge effectiveness. Unless accountability can be measured more intelligently at all levels, I'm not sure the threat bubble can be calmed in a healthy way.

A really useful place to finish – at least in terms of tapping into the 'drive' system for education – is with communications expert Justin Robbins, who, along with Karen Dempster, runs Fit2Communicate – an organisation that works with schools to increase engagement with all stakeholders to enable better student outcomes. Their interest in schools began as parents. What is most empowering about this perspective is that it is tapping into the human dimension of schools – seeing it as an organic entity and not a sterile institution.

---

10. Ofsted and Spielman, A. (2018) *Amanda Spielman speech to the SCHOOLS NorthEast summit* [Transcript]. Available at: www.gov.uk/government/speeches/amanda-spielman-speech-to-the-schools-northeast-summit (Accessed 11 Oct 2018).

What are your thoughts on the current issues around teacher recruitment and what do you see as responsible?

Justin: A big part of the problem is the negativity that we hear in the media around how bad it is to be a teacher today. The main reason that people choose to go into teaching is definitely not to become rich, or because it's an easy profession; it's because they want to share what they love and they want to make a difference in the lives of young people. It's an amazing calling. But what I feel is currently happening is that the media is painting such a bleak picture about the state of education that it is causing these newly qualified teachers to question themselves more and more than they should.

I also think that from a recruitment perspective, the narrative we hear and the initiatives that the government are talking about focus too much on the financial incentives. The initiatives talk around bursaries, they talk around things like extra bonuses for certain subject teachers but they don't talk about the kind of development you'll receive or the amazing children you will meet. They don't talk about the support network or the amazing experiences you will have. And they certainly don't reflect how working with these amazing young people will make you laugh, cry, despair and celebrate, while always loving what you are doing. They just tell a story that doesn't necessarily fit with the real motivators behind being a teacher.

Education is probably about 20 years behind in its thinking compared to modern business. What that leads to is this kind of perception that motivation is still very much around financial incentives and that lack of understanding of well-being, engagement and happiness – just feeling proud of what you do every day. These aren't the 'hard-and-fast' things that people are focused on when it comes to talking about teaching. But if you look at what motivates the people joining the workforce today, it's all about 'millennial motivation'. They are motivated by having a voice that is listened to, being able to work flexibly, feeling valued, and making a difference. They want to be paid, of course, but that's not necessarily their main motivator. We need to remember that, at a macro level, what might have motivated people 20, 30, 40 years ago is not what motivates them today.

Are schools in a position to address this then?

Justin: Schools' hands are tied a little bit from a budget perspective if addressing it means spending money on it. But I look at some of the happiest schools in the country that we've seen. The things that make people happy at school aren't driven by having lots of money to spend. It's about recognising differences, recognising the contribution that people make behind that common cause. It's about that lack of inhibition to stand up for what you believe. A smile, a thank-you, a well done; these cost nothing. Somebody in a school has got to be the first mover. Schools need to think about finding ways of identifying and celebrating people's strengths.

We also believe that every school should have some form of measure of staff engagement. It should be mandatory, whether that's mandated through Ofsted or through some other means. And as much as the league tables around performance are shared every year, we should have league tables showing the internal health of our schools. I regularly speak to school leaders about recruitment. Some of them tell me 'We don't have recruitment and retention problems, so everybody must be fine: nobody complains and nobody is leaving.' This is part of the problem. That doesn't mean that people are fine. I think it's a focus on the wrong measures and a lack of understanding of what actually drives some of those measures that is also part of the problem.

How do you think schools can facilitate a healthier working environment then?

Justin: As well as having a measure of engagement as I have already stated, I think there are some very clear steps that need to be taken.

1. Schools should be encouraged to be more accountable to their local community. First and foremost, schools serve the community in which they operate. Think about the impact that MATs should have – that sense of togetherness in a local community where they should be able to work together for the benefit of their local communities. They should be able to identify opportunities to share learning and best practice across schools without the fear that they're in competition with each other. Competition for pupils is a very big thing in all schools that want to fill their places – but again, it is the wrong measure and drives the wrong kind of accountability.

2. Schools and teachers should be properly trained in how they communicate with parents. I don't just mean how to talk to a parent at a parents' evening. It goes way beyond just having that conversation: it's how to engage with parents in the learning of what students are doing so they can support them outside school. And that doesn't mean every parent needs to become an expert in GCSEs. But it does mean they need to know how to support their child outside school. We hear from parents all of the time saying they want specifics about their own child, not generic emails and text messages. They want to know what they can do to specifically support their child. There are plenty of technology solutions available to support schools in terms of channels; but without that understanding and partnership, they may as well be letters left in a school bag for a week.

3. Schools should be evaluated and graded around the teacher experience that they deliver, from the moment that a teacher or a non-teacher reads a job advert, right the way through to where they finally leave – and all that happens in between. The teacher experience goes through the whole process: the on-boarding, how they are introduced to the technology used in school, how they feel when they have classroom challenges and where they can go for support, how they are inspired by their leaders and those around them – including people who have been there a long time. How do schools actually inspire not just newly qualified teachers but also teachers that are new to the school but that may have been teaching for ten years? Ultimately, when they leave, they shouldn't feel like they just disappear into a black hole: they are part of the alumni of a school. They may even come back in the future. Essentially, when they talk to somebody else about an experience at a school, they should be able to talk positively because it's been a great experience. Even if they've had challenges, they've been dealt with in a positive way. So again, it's about having the whole experience as a process which is mapped out and measured, with schools being held accountable for this.

4. There should be national principles defining what good school leadership looks like. Headteachers should have a standard set of competencies and behaviours that they are held accountable for. We see in the media regular stories about business leaders becoming MAT CEOs or taking over in schools where they have zero teaching experience. We believe that's fine as long as they're all held to a standard set of competencies and behaviours that actually reflect the teacher experience. This is the challenge that we see when teachers become headteachers and they haven't been properly equipped with the different competencies and behaviours required for being the school leader.

5. Schools need to look at positive psychology training for every teacher. We need to look at resilience – and the challenges that a teacher faces every day. 'Resilience' means how we manage when we look at all of the things that happen to teachers – both inside and outside of school – that the school isn't aware of. If you add a challenging work environment to an already challenging classroom, that's when we get to a point where teachers just reach breaking point. Even if, at this point, they reach out for support, or they pick up the phone, it's too late. They've gone too far down the track of feeling the pain of it. Positive psychology enables teachers to manage some of those factors in the early days, to recognise some of the issues, to enable empathy and to recognise and manage some of the issues in the students that they teach. I don't mean that they have to suddenly become experts with students in terms of psychology. I just mean they can recognise some of the symptoms that are coming out and not necessarily respond in negative ways.

To what extent is the outcome-driven culture we find ourselves in responsible for the issues we face?

> **Justin:** I think there is definitely an issue right now. But I also believe that school leaders need to be allowed – even encouraged – to put their school team first. They need to show that they won't be a 'victim' of an Ofsted inspection. There are many reasons why a school may not rank at the top of a league table. But what does matter is asking whether the school has happy staff and students who give their best every day. We are all for holding schools and leaders accountable. They have too important a role not to be held accountable. But once again it is the wrong measures driving the wrong behaviours. It feels like a 'blame' culture approach where schools are looking for reasons to explain shortcomings. Schools should be able to proudly celebrate what they stand for and why they are different.

Justin's ideas are especially interesting as they come from a father – and not an employee. His goals are no different from a school's at their core: he wants the best for his child. What is most striking about the ideas is their vibrancy in terms of community and staff relationships. Academic outcomes would be a by-product of this model, rather than remaining a school's sole purpose. On reflection, if you take the ideas of those above together, a theme emerges: an over-reliance on the wrong measures has forced a serious misalignment of our core drivers as a profession. At this level, compassion involves being honest about this, and not blaming or shaming. The truth is, we've lost our identity at a systemic level – there's almost a sense of shame about our core purpose, leading to an over-compensation in terms of outcomes. Yes, we still have brilliant schools that serve communities amazingly well, but I'd argue that these are produced in spite of – rather than because of – our educational infrastructure. At least teachers can choose to leave or stay in the profession; the real shame is for the students that are being mis-served.

B. School leadership

'People may hear your words, but they feel your attitude.'
John C Maxwell

I'll be as blunt as I can be here: accountability measures are crippling the drive and soothe systems of many modern school leaders, and a threat-based agenda is seeping through our schools (some more than others). In terms of creativity, engagement and attracting the right calibre of people to the profession, this is devastating. However we frame the modern context, school leaders are still vulnerable to inspector subjectivity, just as teachers are vulnerable to school leader subjectivity in interpreting Ofsted edicts. This is especially tricky for schools judged as 'requires improvement': on the cusp of the promised land of 'good', yet at risk of relegation to 'special measures', at which point in time job security and the fight for survival become real. Under such threat, what choice do school leaders have other than to highlight their effectiveness through tangible measures to demonstrate that change is either complete or 'coming soon to a school near you'? In some cases, the compulsion to act brings with it inhumanity to perceived underperformance – some colleagues are objectified as barriers and blockers to success.

As a result, the exam factory metaphor has become remarkably apt: notions of productivity, standardisation, performance and measurability have permeated our schools in a way we could never have envisaged. I've always, rather smugly I suppose, called it Ikea flat pack learning:

'It's worked for them, in that area, so it'll work over here. We'll roll it out and make it uniform, then there's no margin for error. All in the name of equal opportunity.' This was not, I believe, Labour's original vision for academies; it probably wasn't even Mr Gove's. This is not to denigrate some of the wonderful work done by academies in historically challenging schools; but I would be stunned if the success in those schools wasn't due largely to the quality of the individuals and the relationships they forged with the stakeholders.

I don't think it's difficult to argue that in the last decade or so, the focus on outcomes has taken some of the character away from the profession, leaving less space for warmth and compassion – both for oneself and for others. Rutger Bregman's *Utopia for Realists* coins the term 'mental bandwidth', asking why poorer people are often susceptible to making 'bad' decisions. For example, if we are worrying about whether we'll be able to put food on the table to feed our families, we'll be less concerned about buying organic tender-stemmed broccoli twice a week. Well, I'd argue that too much mental bandwidth in schools is often taken up by threat, leaving less time and space for warmth, caring and soothe (let alone our all-important core purpose). When I spoke with Mary Myatt on this, her words were especially interesting.

What inhibitors are there to schools 'living out' their values?

Mary: There are times when it is easier to take the quicker steps. For instance, getting good grades in Year 6 and Year 11. But we need to catch ourselves. For leaders, we should never forget that everyone we're dealing with is a human being first and a professional second. We should remind ourselves (and the settings that we lead on a regular basis) why we're in this game. When we look to the bigger purpose of schools, they've all got their statements and ambitions. If those are worthwhile then they ought to be revisited every now and then – at least once a half-term. That daily grind can *really be* a daily grind. Acting morally doesn't mean to say we're going to be perfect but it means we do need a regular dose of injecting ourselves with why we are doing this work.

What about the pressures from the wider system?

Mary: One of the things that can happen is that we can get stuck into a less helpful narrative. The DfE (Department for Education), Ofsted – the point is they are there and it can't be denied that they add additional pressure on schools. So that pressure has to be managed. My view is that if we are doing the right things by our pupils, then it is likely to align with accountability. If we spend too much time moaning about accountability and external expectations then what some of this does is to remove some of the capacity – both within myself and others who hear me talk like that – for making change within my setting. We mustn't make them an excuse for actually just cracking on.

Mary's words here are honest and hopeful – unsurprisingly. A useful place to build from would be how school leaders recruit, develop and retain their staff. The recent report from the NFER (National Foundation for Education Research) – *Teacher Workforce Dynamics* – equates high leaving rates in teachers not to age, but to experience, indicating a need for higher levels of support in the early stages. Professor Glazzard's concerns (below) about teacher training seem well founded, especially in light of the Education Datalab's work on 'sausage-machine schools'[11] that recruit a disproportionate number of inexperienced and inexpensive teachers to fill staffing gaps, but see these teachers burning out within five years of being in the profession. This is particularly the case in schools based in areas of disadvantage that are naturally more likely to be stressful. It's not about bashing these schools and their teachers: it's about asking the right questions and providing the right levels of support for leaders to prevent them from using these strategies (either consciously or subconsciously). If they can't then see the moral shortcomings of this approach, then yes, give them a bashing.

One can see the attraction of a culture that produces 'evidence' of compliance and indications that learning is happening (although science tells us something entirely different about learning and long-term memory). As an example of a collection of poor learning proxies, Tom

---

11. Staufenberg, J. (2017) 'Revealed: the "sausage-machine schools" pushing new teachers out the profession', *Schools Week* [Online]. Available at: www.bit. ly/2sTlBz9 (Accessed 5 Oct 2018).

Sherrington's wonderful blog post '10 low impact activities to do less of – or stop altogether'[12] hits the nail on the head beautifully. These are the post's main recommendations:

1. Subject report comments: STOP

2. Performance management documentation: STRIP BACK

3. Data drops: DO LESS

4. Logging 'can do' statements in centralised tracking systems: STOP

5. Grading lessons or book scrutinies: STOP

6. Self-assessment reflection sheets: www/ebi STOP

7. Written comments in books: DO MUCH LESS

8. Detailed lesson plans: STOP

9. Detailed school development plans: STRIP BACK

10. Producing original teaching resources: DO LESS

Again, I've no doubt that some of these things probably had a decent grounding in terms of rationale, once upon a time. Some of these things maybe even worked, but probably worked because once upon a time they had someone with real credibility and integrity thinking them up, not because of the strategy itself. Again, there is a lack of understanding about external and internal motivational forces. The so-called 'transparency' argument about outcomes and justifications has, in my view, led to leaders becoming wholly reductionist in their approach to what they want to see in their schools. And as outlined above, a threat-addled brain will be seriously inhibited when it comes to creatively and reflectively solving problems.

Now would be a useful time to bring in the thoughts of Jill Berry – a headteacher for ten years, and now a leadership consultant. Her ideas are profound yet eminently sensible and workable.

---

12. Sherrington, T. (2017) '10 low impact activities to do less of – or stop altogether', *Teacherhead* [Blog]. Available at: www.bit.ly/2GaRuLk (Accessed 5 Oct 2018).

What are your views on the influence of outcomes over education?

Jill: I think making very high-level judgements based on data is an incredibly blunt tool, and I think it's heartening that Ofsted are not just looking at results but also looking more broadly at the curriculum and the educational provision within the classroom and beyond. That's a really positive move. I just hope that translates to a real difference in terms of how schools are held accountable. Otherwise it's loaded, because outcomes will depend on so many factors beyond your control.

Inevitably if schools are under such pressure then it is going to lead to some gaming, and I think it is hard for the government to be very critical about schools doing things that aren't exactly ethical when we consider how much is at stake. We need to look at what we are trying to do in schools – what *really* matters – and how we can make sure that schools are held accountable for those things. We've got to move away from a blame culture. If you've got fear then it leads to a blame culture – leaders are fearful and stressed and they communicate that to everyone else. It takes a very brave school leader to say 'This isn't right in my context and it's not aligned with our fundamental principles.' When you're a new leader, you tend to do as you're told and that's led to unintended consequences.

It's becoming more stressful and less compassionate: high stakes, high threat. So we've got to break out of that and go back to basic humanitarian principles in terms of how we treat each other and respect each other. If there are problems and there is some underperformance, we need to have a dialogue: we need to have reflection, we need to be looking at development and support; not just judging people, labelling them, blaming them, getting rid of them and trying to bring in someone new. That's just papering over the cracks. It is about *supporting* the people we've got: I like the appreciative inquiry idea where we look at what's working and how we can do *more* rather than just thinking of what's broken, side-lining people and getting them out. We need to be much more positive about the strength in the profession and how we can build on it rather than trying to just root out weakness.

Are we doing enough to support all stakeholders?

Jill: I think not. And I think that's because of the pressure people are under. There are a lot of people with very good intentions. I think politicians have the best intentions. There are also a lot of people who are committed to closing the social mobility gap and doing the best for children in disadvantaged circumstances. I don't think anybody out there is necessarily callous and uncaring. I think Michael Gove wanted to do what's best for young people; but how we've gone about it in many respects has been misguided, and certainly trying to pit schools against each other in a competition has been a failure. We need to look at collaboration, cooperation and supporting each other so it isn't every school for itself. We have a responsibility to *all* children, so what can we do to raise standards for everybody rather than it just being about our own school? I think there needs to be a greater selflessness: not sticking up a banner outside of school saying we are 'outstanding' or 'good.' If the school down the road is struggling, we need to think about what we can do to help them and that's what is needed. If you're trying to raise money for shareholders, then that's a particular context; but if you're trying to improve people's lives then that is far more complex and nuanced. We've got to reduce the threat, and we've got to focus on growth – not end product and measuring schools, departments and teachers against one another. Everybody can have poor days and struggle, and a recognition of that is important – we're not intrinsically 'outstanding' or 'weak.'

Being a school leader is an important job, but a job it isn't *all* that we are. And I felt very strongly that I loved being a head, and I enjoyed it; but I realised I didn't want to do it for 20 years. I always knew that when I stopped being head there would still be a *person* left behind. My professional identity was not the same as my personal identity and I always had a life beyond my job, and relationships, friends, hobbies and interests and I think that made me stronger. Since I stopped being a head, I've certainly made sure that I lead a very rich, full and interesting life. So it is about *balance*. It's about *sustainability*; I think if people can't do their job well enough without sacrificing their relationships or their mental health then there's something very badly wrong. And when you're a leader, I think you have to model the fact that it's possible to get the balance right and for it to be sustainable. If you're actually sending out the wrong message because you think you have to work every minute of every day, that doesn't make you a successful leader – it makes you an exhausted leader.

What are the biggest influences on teacher recruitment and retention?

Jill: I have to say I think leadership is really important and it's one of the reasons I want to work with leaders at all levels, because your leader can make a huge difference to your morale and your satisfaction and your feeling that you're in control of your professional life. I've done some reading about the stress of teaching, and it's not just workload – it's feeling out of control and being in a professional context where you don't have sufficient agency. You feel like you are being manipulated or controlled by others. Workload will be a part of it: when you have more than you can cope with and nobody's listening to you or helping you, and they are unrealistic in their expectations. Middle leaders are really important because for most of us, in terms of our day-to-day professional practice, our middle leaders have a significant impact on how we feel, whether we're enjoying it and whether we feel we are achieving. Leadership varies a lot, though. There are a lot of good leaders out there, but there are some that are fearful and passing on the stress and pressure rather than helping to filter that pressure and actually enabling the people in their teams to build capacity and to grow in confidence. They're actually making the job harder by really piling on the pressure.

We need to have a better narrative about teaching. It's appreciative inquiry again, and what's going well, and how we can *celebrate* it. We need to be making sure that leaders at all levels know their value, as well as knowing and valuing their teams, and giving them what they need to grow and develop and be stronger. I do meet disaffected teachers from time to time through my work and I've written about this in my blog. If you are really unhappy, try a change of school. But if you feel teaching isn't working for you, it may just be a particular school in that particular context or an ethos that isn't bringing out the best in you, and I know so many people who have had a change of school and rediscovered the love of their subject – usually, it's because they're being *led* more successfully. If leaders were stronger and we recognised that we've got more agency than we often give ourselves credit for, I think we would be a stronger profession.

So, do you think that the system – and I mean the infrastructure in education – is allowing that to happen at the moment?

Jill: No – I think we're too ad hoc in terms of preparation and development of leaders. Although the NPQH (National Professional Qualification for Headship) had its faults, we were the first country in the world to have a mandatory qualification for school leaders, and I think that was a very positive step. So I think we need to be a bit more systematic about identifying potential leaders, then developing them and bringing them on and supporting them once they're in role. I was very sad about the National College of Teaching and Leadership (what it became after NCSL) being absorbed into the DfE, and I think having a national college dedicated to school leadership is a really important statement about its importance. At the moment, I don't think the infrastructure or the systems are right – the emphasis isn't right. Leaders need to be dedicated to helping teachers to be the best they can be.

Jill's thoughts were especially interesting if we think about the inhibitors of compassion in schools, and the significance of having a core purpose. Bravery in leaders is a common theme that occurs throughout the interviews – and I think bravery can only really happen when someone has appropriate levels of 'threat', 'drive' and 'soothe'. In our context, 'bravery' stems not from running from predators and feeling threatened, but it stems from feeling safe and valued – in other words, soothed. I mention soothe here because this is, effectively, the compassion part. When we have compassion for another, it grows organically. In the short term, our own mental health improves; but in the longer term, our compassion for somebody gives them the space to have compassion for others as well. But at the moment, this is stifled by the weeds of fear and threat.

It's useful to get the experience and thoughts of individuals on the front line right now. Tudor Griffiths – headteacher at Kettlethorpe High School in Wakefield for 13 years (and before that at Wortley High School in Leeds for four years) – kindly gave his time to discuss the current educational climate.

How has the job changed since you became a headteacher?

Tudor: A lot has changed in relation to strategic thinking and planning for the longer game than when I first started. My current role is much more about the strategic direction of the school, spending time thinking about what is happening in the next year. Budgets are massively under pressure, and that causes considerable pressure in terms of the day-to-day running of the school. Unfortunately budgets have been really cut back over many years. Two or three years ago, for example, the capital grant money that we used to get would be around £200,000; now we are talking sums of £30,000 a year.

It is also a much more dynamic and fluid landscape to lead within. When I first started, you were a headteacher and you were assisted by the local authority. Now you have to do that and work alongside MATs and a changing landscape of different providers and different ways of working. It's no longer an education-based model; it has more links with business and therefore you are beginning to see sharp business practices coming into play. I think we have taken the worst out of business in terms of negative working practices, which are fairly ruthless. They are very tight, with harder accountability and a lack of opportunity to develop and sustain a role. If you cannot do it, you are out very quickly.

The pressures always increase. People in headship struggle with the amount of responsibility and the increased accountability around it. The Progress 8, GCSE results. At any given point in any year, 50% of teachers are underperforming because they are falling below the Progress 8 measure. It is lonelier than it ever was.

We are not making biscuits and manufacturing; we are building up skills for life. And I think that the whole ethos and values of a school are much more than just the end results in terms of exam results. It is how children feel and whether they have the confidence and skills to move forward. Can they be independent? Can they make choices? Can they be kind and trustworthy? Those things that make good people.

Where do you see the balance between accountability and humanity?

Tudor: Increasingly within the profession, we have seen that some leaders have lost their moral purpose and they are unethical in the way they practise, the way they work, and the way they treat staff and pupils. The culture of 'offrolling' and the idea that it is acceptable to take children out of a school and deny them the opportunity to have an educational experience in their own local community – I think it is totally wrong. There is a real sense of responsibility for the profession as a whole here to make sure that we model the best ways of working for young colleagues coming through. As you join the profession – and you join leadership particularly – you see good practice in what leaders do, and that will hopefully help. This is a responsibility, as is the responsibility of re-educating those leaders in schools that have gone off the track morally. Unfortunately, there are no longer as many autonomous headteachers because many school leaders are accountable to CEOs and therefore they have got to play a difficult game of meeting the needs of the school as well as satisfying a taskmaster or an overseer. We are in a very interesting landscape at the moment and hopefully there are enough high-quality individuals and leaders out there to make a difference. There is a whole discussion to be had around ethos and values and curriculum and *why* you do it. That is a nice place to start in schools.

Something that really resonates from this discussion is the theme of clarity and purpose around what we do. If you map this upwards to schools as a whole, there's a sense that schools are trying to do *everything* but doing it badly – whilst not thinking about their core purpose. Inevitably, obsession with outcomes leads to less space for other things – it's simple mathematics. Here, I am sure you will agree, it comes back to honesty and self-reflection, which is what we need to try and create the space for. As we move towards the end of this section, it's really important to again recognise solutions. I asked Dame Alison Peacock her thoughts on enhancing staff well-being:

What did you do to influence positive change in your school?

Alison: As a headteacher what made a difference to me – in terms of my capacity to lead and then to try to lead beyond the school – was employing an art therapist that came into school for half a day a week. I often had members of staff or children – people who needed some expert input – come to me to say that things are difficult, and through transference you can just absorb all of that. But I could see it was something that was going to wear me out. I also had a member of staff who we paid to do a postgraduate qualification in therapeutic studies. That meant that I then I got someone else who was able (whilst having supervision herself) to be involved in supporting people who were finding things difficult. I'm someone who wants to fix things, but sometimes there isn't anything you can actually do other than listen, and that's exhausting. It's not that I didn't then have a role as a leader, but it wasn't my sole responsibility to be the person that people came to when things were difficult.

Pushing away a problem or putting things under the carpet won't solve it. When I went to Wroxham, I said, 'This is going to become a listening school.' Once you establish that, people will come and talk to you. That pays hugely in terms of how you engage your community, how you enable people to flourish, how you create an environment where everybody's learning journey is important – not just the children but the entire staff team and also families. People will come to you. And what began to happen was I realised I needed other people to do some of that really deep listening so that we could go beyond just saying we're a 'listening school' and make sure that we were acting on things people were bringing to us. I also realised that I personally was becoming worn down by it all; I couldn't hold everything. There's something about that humility where you realise that you haven't got all the answers but you seek to find other people that can help.

I've done some work around 'teaching without limits'. It's not about saying 'Let me find out what's wrong with you' but about saying 'How can I as a teacher find a way to help you learn?' It's another way of looking that is far more enabling and far more powerful. It doesn't assume a deficit; it assumes a *complexity*. The job of being a teacher is incredibly difficult and challenging but also joyful. The stress comes when the challenge outweighs the moments of being able to celebrate those successful moments.

What are your views on the notion of toxic schools?

Alison: What we're talking about here – and it doesn't have to be within a school – is any culture that is dominated by a bullying presence that means that people can't behave as they would want to. But for me, the only way to get the best out of people is the balance between really high expectations and, essentially, love. Your best success is when people thrive. If you feel you're being bullied and demeaned, and if you lose your dignity and you're being called out, it demotivates you. It may initially result in people sitting up a bit straighter, but after that it leads to demoralisation. The increasing prevalence of those characters that create that toxic culture are often in situations themselves where *they* feel under threat. There are structures and demands that cause our leaders of leaders to behave in this way.

The whole reason for my moving from being a headteacher – the job I loved – to the Chartered College is because my style of leadership is the style that we've been describing, which is one of enabling the flourishing of success, driven by a really strong desire to make things better for the profession. There's a rigorous underpinning that says we need to know what we're talking about. We need to present as professionals; we need to have pride in what we do. But this all comes as part of creating a culture where you feel good as a participant because you are working hard, you can see the outcomes of what you're doing and you know what you're doing is contributing something worthwhile. The opposite to that is you're working very hard but you can't see any outcomes that you value. You can see sheets and sheets of data that you filled in but you don't believe they have any meaning. It doesn't top you up, it just drags you further down.

Again, another theme we can recognise is around humility and self-awareness, as well as placing warmth and – yes – compassion at the heart of everything we do. It feels as if Dame Alison achieved success by framing the agenda around her school in a positive and warm light. Consistency and clarity are key, but it surely has to be practised with warmth.

C. A teacher's life

'Mental health is produced socially: the presence or absence of mental health is above all a social indicator and therefore requires social, as well as individual solutions.'

World Health Organisation

Teachers are not trying to increase the value of shares; they are trying to develop young minds. That requires sensitivity and empathy as well as strength. It raises the question: are the very things that make us great teachers actually making us more vulnerable in the present context? I discussed this with Dr Emma Kell, who has done wonderful work on the notion of 'toxic schools'. Her perspective on this is especially interesting, as she has experience of leading at senior level as well as leading from the middle:

Could you tell me a bit about how the notion of 'toxic schools' came about?

Emma: I would say I was very lucky in the first 15 or 16 years of my career. I think around the time I came into teaching, there was a real sense of optimism and excitement in schools. There were battles over funding and academisation but there was a real sense of 'work hard, play hard'. Then I jumped out of a school and into a post without properly researching it and without trusting my instincts. Suffice to say that the school and I simply weren't compatible in terms of our values or approaches; and like any dysfunctional relationship, it had a catastrophic effect on my well-being and led me to rethinking my commitment to the teaching profession.

The Teacher Gap talks about 100 schools, but I think we're talking quite a lot more. When I sent out quite a vague message asking for teachers' experiences of toxic schools, I received 250 email responses in two weeks. I quite like the way you're focusing on compassion because you're flipping it on its head and making it something positive. Currently, trust – and the erosion of trust – is a key issue; people are micromanaged to within an inch of their lives. Teachers don't mind working hard, but they want a level of autonomy, and I think a lot of teachers are feeling very voiceless at the moment.

What does the future hold? Do we have an understanding of the longer-term impact?

Emma: I am incredibly worried. Look at any of the data from the NFER or the Wellbeing Index: we've seen this coming, we've been banging on about this for years when we were all on strike in the early 2000s. That's the most frustrating thing. As things stand, whilst there a lot of people doing things individually, somebody needs to join these up and get the voice into Westminster. It does feel as if there is an increasing sense of urgency but I'm not sure if it's reaching the right people yet. The budget was a real slap in the face. The comment about the 'little extras like mini buses' said a lot.[13]

More disturbingly, there's this new layer of cynicism and resignation. Teachers are moving from being outraged to being exhausted. They think there's no point saying anything because nothing happens. Some research has shown that teachers are less interested in their own professional development because they're just exhausted. That's dangerous: you then get people going to work simply for the salary to pay the bills and the mortgage.

---

13. Schofield, K. and Bates, L. (2018) 'Philip Hammond says extra budget cash for schools was "nice gesture" following backlash', *PoliticsHome* [Online]. Available at: www.bit.ly/2TmwIMz (Accessed 1 Nov 2018).

Do you think that toxic schools are an indication of an uncertainty about what the point of education actually is?

Emma: Well yes. You're back to that idea of 'measure what you value, don't value what you measure'. That's a huge question: have we lost what we're actually trying to do because we're so conditioned now? I hate to say it, but I think we have. We've got into some terrible habits: most middle leaders admit to relying too much on book scrutinies and turning up to meetings without a vast array of impact data – getting things ticked off for the sake of doing them rather than in the interest of their core purpose. It does make me question what it's for. Maybe we need to look at models elsewhere and find out. It's almost as if any impact on students as human beings is an unexpected bonus: we tick the PSHE box on our lesson-planning pro formas (the lesson-planning pro formas that Ofsted say we don't need to do) but are we actually thinking about developing those whole children? Or are we going back to old O levels and prioritising cramming for exams? Not only has creativity been squeezed out of the curriculum, but it has been squeezed out of the very essence of teachers' personas.

Again, mapping this onto the CFT model is incredibly interesting. Wonderful though it is as an intrinsic pursuit, education still uses a mammalian ranking and status index to judge schools, even though – surprising as it may seem – we've developed a whole new layer of brain in the last two million years. Emma's point of view demonstrates the impact not only on the middle but in the classroom as well. In terms of the end results of this, the salient facts are the following. From the 775 teachers surveyed by Professor Jonathan Glazzard:

- 81% reported that poor mental health negatively impacted on the quality of relationships with their learners.
- 54% reported poor mental health.
- 52% reported that their illness had been identified by a GP.

Building on this, the NFER's report referred to above summarised its primary findings as follows:

Rising pupil numbers, shortfalls in the number of trainee teachers and concerns about the proportion of teachers who say they are considering leaving the profession means that teacher supply in the state sector is a major policy issue in England.

Looking at the projections alone, we are in dire straits. Since 2010, the number leaving teaching has increased – more so than in other frontline public services such as nursing and policing. The research details the reasons given for leaving, noting the influence of high workload, driven by policy change and inspection demands. In MATs, the proportion of teachers leaving was found to be higher too, just as the risk of leaving increased with teachers working in Ofsted-graded 'inadequate' schools. This is before we even get to the issue of retaining and training of quality practitioners, an aspect of research the report itself acknowledges is 'beyond the scope of this research'. Teaching now has a younger age profile than both nursing and policing. And there will definitely be links between age and lack of experience as a predictor for leaving the profession, too.

Effectively, the problems are twofold: not only is the profession haemorrhaging in numbers, but simultaneously struggling to attract, train and retain a sufficient calibre of professionals. This interview with Professor Glazzard allows us to dig a little deeper into what the data is telling us. It's important to keep this in mind in terms of the CFT-linked discussions that follow:

Could you summarise your own findings and maybe what you took away from the research in your own words?

Jonathan: What teachers said to me was unanimous: they felt that their mental ill health had a detrimental impact on the quality of their teaching, on pupils' learning, on pupils' progress and on relationships with children – and with colleagues as well. Teachers felt they were snappy, irritable, and had less patience with children because of the way they were feeling. They felt it was actually making them less able to form relationships with children. They also indicated that it was beginning to negatively influence their relationships with colleagues: some of them talked about wanting to withdraw from social situations and isolating themselves within the school.

What would you say we can do to support teachers more effectively?

Jonathan: When I interviewed the teachers I was obviously able to probe a bit more and find out the reasons behind the causes of teacher mental ill health. The survey was really finding out about the impacts of teacher mental health on pupils, staff, teaching and learning; but the interviews were about trying to find out the causes.

I expected that workload would manifest as the biggest issue because that's the issue we hear about all the time and that's the issue the government is addressing. But actually, teachers didn't say that to me. They knew teaching was going to be hard work; they signed up to teaching and knew that was the case. It's not about workload. What they said was that they could cope with the workload, the planning, marking assessment feedback or even student behaviour if the culture in the school was supportive – if they felt trusted and supported by colleagues and by leaders in the school. So it's fundamentally about the school *culture*. They were talking about not feeling trusted; they were talking about being endlessly micromanaged through lesson observations and learning walks. Constantly being held accountable for pupil progress – that's the thing that really caused them significant stress. It's about the incessant accountability that's placed on them, and that lack of trust from senior leaders. They didn't feel able to shape their job roles and they didn't feel in control; they felt that they were simply told what to do and how to teach – these were fundamentally the key issues. It's about the cultures that exist within schools stemming from leadership teams.

To what extent do you blame senior leaders for this? Do you think this is the fault of the senior leaders or something bigger?

Jonathan: I think it's difficult because senior leaders are also under pressure to raise standards. Senior leaders are controlled by Ofsted, the government, the DfE, local authorities, CEOs of MATs. That pressure transfers down onto teachers and then down onto children. Having said that, senior leaders are able to shape the culture of a school – they are the key people who can make a school happy, that can create a positive culture within the school. I accept that there is pressure on them; but actually if staff are happy under an inclusive culture and they feel respected, surely they'll do a better job and raise standards anyway.

Did you think academies are the cause of this?

Jonathan: That's a tricky one because academies aren't all the same. In some cases, everything is the same across all the different schools. Some actually give the schools individuality. However, I think there are enough examples now of the kind of chains with some very dubious practices. I'm not going to name them but we know that there are academy chains where staff are let go if their faces don't fit. And there's plenty of examples of moving children around schools within MATs, and offrolling – that type of thing. So I think they contribute. We probably need to do more research on it though.

What else are you going to look into in the future?

Jonathan: I'm interested in exploring what's actually going on with NQTs at the moment. In the recent *Teacher Wellbeing Index*,[14] the teachers that have been in the profession for between one and five years experience more mental health issues than teachers who've been teaching longer than that. We need to find out what's going on with new teachers. Do these issues arise because they lack resilience or because they're now going into an education system that doesn't allow them to grow and develop as teachers and allows them to make mistakes and learn from their mistakes? I think we also need to find out more because in the green paper[15] the government don't acknowledge any of the factors that might contribute to young people's mental health such as the exam system, the lack of curriculum choice and the academic nature of the curriculum. I think that needs to be researched more as a way of actually presenting some of this evidence to the government.

14. Education Support Partnership (2018) *Teacher wellbeing index 2018*. Available at: www.bit.ly/2Uy4crz (Accessed 24 Oct 2018).
15. Department of Health and Department for Education (2017) *Transforming children and young people's mental health provision: a green paper*. London: The Stationery Office.

We might also need to look more at teacher training courses. When I talk to teachers they tell me that things are very different from previously. I qualified to be a teacher 20 years ago. Things are different, things are challenging and we now have more and more children coming through with *very* low starting points, more and more children with behavioural needs. What we do in teacher training is just pop more and more into it, rather than focusing on the quality or its key components. It gets to a point where you're doing things but not doing them very *effectively.* You're trying to tick boxes to say you've done that. And I think we need to be thinking about a fundamental part of training and looking at how teachers can manage, and how they can manage stress and anxiety. You can't do that in a one-hour lecture or half an hour.

Professor Glazzard places a lot of emphasis on senior leaders, and rightly so. For now, although there's lots of work and reflection to be done on emotional intelligence, it's not about expecting everyone to be emotional geniuses; it's about acknowledging the complexities of the human experience within a school environment, and at least showing willing to empathise with others. Again, core purpose and values really strike at the heart of what's going wrong currently; but they also offer potential solutions too. We can't dismiss the stresses and pressures on senior leaders, but we can ask them to ask more intelligent questions of the teaching that they witness. From a CFT perspective, as I will discuss below, there is a difference between preference and judgement. Even when something happens in a classroom that leaders don't feel happy with, threatening and punitive conversations and actions will almost certainly shut down any sense of control and agency for those being observed – thereby effectively guaranteeing that the outcome of the conversation won't be favourable anyway. What follows is an articulation – from the ground level – linking the CFT model to the life of a modern teacher.

First and foremost, teaching is an incredible profession. But given its nature, it can be very lonely and very isolating. Whilst prior to 2014, a teacher's salary would rise in line with experience, a teacher is now subject to meeting performance management targets (or a headteacher's discretion?) if their pay is to rise. Again, in order to justify decisions, targets are often made measurable, resulting in data-driven targets which meet the school's need. With my CFT hat on, I can speak with absolute credibility around this issue: an arbitrary target (often only assigned to exam classes) does provide me with an incentive to work harder only insofar as I do not wish to feel like a failure in myself – I don't want to have 'failed my performance management'. In Daniel Pink's book *Drive*, he discusses precisely this. Now, assuming that teachers (having made the decision to move into the profession) are happy with their salary, his words are particularly interesting:

> Carrots and sticks can achieve precisely the opposite of their intended aims. Mechanisms designed to increase motivation can dampen it. Tactics aimed at boosting creativity can reduce it. Programs to promote good deeds can make them disappear. Meanwhile, instead of restraining negative behaviour, rewards and punishments can often set it loose – and give rise to cheating, addiction, and dangerously myopic thinking.[16]

Threat is the only possible way of interpreting a failure to 'move up' the pay spine: either my work has not been respected and valued, or school budgets are insufficient and the school can't afford it, making the situation altogether more unfair anyway. My point is this: seemingly 'transparent' strategies around measurability and performance have put a peculiar kind of distortion on the way schools place value on teachers' work, which – in the context of mental health – is dangerous. Not only this, but replicated systems and processes can be dropped in from elsewhere end up enhancing paper work with little real emphasis placed on the genuine valuation of creativity (that is, our drive and soothe systems).

Should I be expected to be able to have a sensible discussion about my classes? Perhaps an honest and open reflection on my planning and my books? Of course. But it needn't require extensive paperwork and evidence portfolio collection (in some cases). It is important for leaders and teachers to act with intelligence, credibility and integrity, and

---

16. Pink, D. (2011) *Drive: the surprising truth about what motivates us.* Edinburgh: Canongate Books.

the current system encourages none of these things. Gilbert himself discusses the difficulties of individuals living simply on the 'drive-threat axis' which in the short term might be functional, but in the long term is unsustainable, leading to behaviours linked with pride/narcissism/ uncaring – take your pick.

Reflecting back on Pink's words – and the types of motivation now (even inadvertently) employed by many schools – I'd suggest that the rigidity of the modern framework for the evaluation of school performance lends itself to highly repetitive, monotonous, mechanical and boring tasks; but not so much for creativity, longevity and commitment in the long term. The statistics bear this out. The modern context of education encourages schools – perhaps even without them knowing – to produce cultures that represent precisely this. Teachers aren't stupid. Whether they will receive their performance-related pay – and whether they will even (more importantly) feel valued in their schools – is all too often linked with a learning walk, a drop in, and anecdotal evidence about what they happen to be doing that day. Schools need to demonstrate that they are fully aware of the quality of teaching going on in their classrooms, creating the need for Excel databases and traffic lighting. It is a perverse irony that by storming classrooms and judging teachers so punitively, school leaders are inadvertently undermining (perhaps in some cases crushing) teachers – all the while claiming to be acting in the interest of students, who so desperately rely on confident and competent teachers. Fundamentally, what we are left with is the fact that an intensely human occupation now often has an intensely threat-based context. In some cases, teachers will even begin to wrongly interpret innocuous actions and gestures, feeling undermined and threatened even when leaders don't intend them to. Indeed, we also have to reflect upon what kind of teachers such rigid and punitive structures are producing, and what they are asking us to place value upon as we move forward as professionals day by day.

More specifically, the CFT model gives us four 'motivational systems' linked with how we see ourselves in relation to others. It's worth reflecting upon how each of these relate to us as individuals in our own contexts. Each is considered here in turn:

1. Competing and social ranking

The implications of competition have already been mentioned, but in terms of their teachers, ministers and schools need to ask themselves: 'What do we value?' If the answer is something more complex than student outcomes (which it should be) then it makes no sense to measure teacher performance only by exam results and other things with only external appearance. And 'we have no other measures' is no excuse.

We compare and rank ourselves against others. Ragging staff and judging them against poor proxies for learning is hardly conducive to fostering a healthy self-view amongst staff. Although we can never force anyone to learn anything, Dylan Wiliam points out that 'our classrooms seem to be based on the opposite principle – that if they try really hard, teachers can do the learning for the learners. This is only exacerbated by accountability regimes that mandate sanctions for teachers, schools, and for districts, but not for students.'[17] Our education system is based on the same principle.

One MAT I know of circulates residuals of individual colleagues throughout departments, and also shares subject-based residuals in whole-staff meetings. Inadvertently, such practice taps into an incredibly old processing system in the minds of staff – a processing system (with threat and drive at its core, rather than soothe and drive) that is inadvertently doing more harm than good. Again, winning/losing scenarios on a school-wide scale are likely to foster heightened anxiety amongst all stakeholders, but in an altogether more sinister twist, constant experience of 'defeat' and 'failure' is well documented to lead to depression. Please don't think I'm suggesting that depression will spread school-wide: I would, however, say that such cultures heighten the risk at the individual level, but almost certainly cause paralysis at the team level. Again, this isn't about removal of accountability; it's about a guarantee of what will *not* work.

---

17. Wiliam, D. (2018) *Embedded formative assessment.* Bloomington, IN: Solution Tree Press.

2. Cooperation/sharing

It's well documented that our desire to share and solve problems together starts at a very, very young age.[18] As humans, we love it, and we're wired for it. One only need look at the explosion of teachers taking to Twitter to share and support one another. Perhaps one of the best examples of this is #TeamEnglish, with initiatives such as the Lit Drive[19] (thank you, Kat Howard), which has tapped into not only people's creativity and passion, but their hunger for sharing and cooperation in the name of workload reduction and student progress. This is a wonderful example of collaboration in an entirely drive-based and neutral context. As CFT would say: a shift from 'me-ness to we-ness'. I'd argue that in schools, simply taking a picture of someone's lesson and putting it on a PowerPoint slide once a week in staff briefings hardly constitutes actually fostering a culture of cooperation and sharing.

I'm not sure how teachers are supposed to cooperate and share with one another when teaching at their maximum number of allocated hours and doing goodness knows what else in the course of a week. And it's not just about teaching and learning: it's about all those small things between departments and areas of the school that come together and are so much more than the sum of their parts. Ultimately, schools have to make space and truly place not just these behaviours at the heart of everything they do, but the values behind them. And they should not start with the behaviour of 'good practice' and hope that seeing a picture will magically lead to more brilliant examples of this.

3. Caring and nurturing

Yes, self-care is vital. But it is basically preservation, and it doesn't really tap into what makes us human. And education is an intrinsically human pursuit. Our ability to care for others is altogether more important here. Empathy is bloody hard work. It's about getting into the hole with the other person, rather than

---

18. Tomasello, M. and Vaish, A. (2013) 'Origins of human cooperation and horality', *Annual Review of Psychology* 64 (1) pp. 231–255.

19. www.litdrive.org.uk

standing at the top, shouting down, 'Yeah, looks awful down there. I feel sorry for you!'

At one stage when I was feeling particularly depressed, my wife burst into tears: 'I'm so compassion-fatigued, I've got nothing left to give. I can barely stay afloat myself!' I felt awful. Sadly, the Education Support Partnership's *Teacher Wellbeing Index* (surveying 1187 staff) found that 80% of the senior leaders surveyed described themselves as 'stressed'. So just how much have our senior leaders actually got to give?

In the present culture in education, it's important to question how many resources – emotional, financial, time, logistic – schools are able to give to their staff and students. It's no good *saying* it; it's about actually placing it front and centre. Having high expectations need not mean behaving in a way that can be deemed inhumane. If you have the integrity and the intelligence to engage in a conversation about performance, then you shouldn't need brute force. Myatt again makes this point brilliantly:

> When the tone of a setting has been underpinned by 'humans first, professionals second', something interesting happens. People are happy to be held to account. This is because they want to do their best work.[20]

I find it profoundly interesting that Myatt hits on something that speaks with direct relevance to the CFT model. There is very much a scientific basis to what she says.

4. Seeking and responding to care

The benefits of care and nurture are massive – so massive that we are wired to seek and respond to being cared for. In the face of the inescapable distress that school environments naturally create, caring for colleagues and one another can be everything. Recognising the stresses of the environment and recognising the natural reactions in one another is not a choice, but the *only* choice in the present context. Empathy is a difficult thing to hold

20. Myatt, M. (2016a) *High challenge, low threat: finding the balance*. Woodbridge: John Catt Educational Ltd.

in one's mind (especially when feeling threatened), but without it, the behaviour of others can feel unpredictable and chaotic. Place this in the inherently chaotic environment of a school and we have a problem. Of course, another layer to this is the issue of identification: it is easier to be compassionate and empathetic for those we identify with, adding another layer of subjectivity into the equation. There is no hiding from this. *The Teacher Wellbeing Index*[21] summarises:

> Although many education professionals are broadly satisfied and happy with their lives, a worrying 76% have disclosed they have experienced a range of symptoms where work was a contributing factor (75% in 2017). Rising levels of insomnia and irritability/ mood swings over the last year are the most common features.

When we feel wanted and respected, there is an actual chemical payoff in the brain (a chemical called oxytocin). Mental health issues are often caused and reinforced by shame and loneliness – before we even start, it can feel like schools propagate these feelings naturally. Schools need to ask themselves what they are doing in order to promote care. How are they showing teachers and students that care is meaningful and a key part of the culture they experience every day?

In the *Wellbeing Index*, there is one key finding that I think speaks to this particularly meaningfully, again indicating a common theme. When teachers were asked about how educational institutions can improve the mental health and well-being of their workforce, in a repeat of the previous year's findings, by far the most popular response was line managers working with them to reduce workload (54%, as opposed to 53% in 2017). There is something to this, I think. It links to having the credibility and integrity to take ownership (with others) of priorities in line with values. As teachers, we have a degree of responsibility for the learning of our students. In essence, I think it's important not to throw everything at someone and say 'over to you'; it's about guidance rather than unilateral feedback. Interestingly, the

21. Education Support Partnership (2018) *Teacher wellbeing index 2018*. Available at: www.bit.ly/2Uy4crz (Accessed 24 Oct 2018).

second biggest influencer on this survey was communication around change – something we have plenty of control over in our schools. Care, then, needn't be about giving everyone an additional five hours of free time a week, but about acknowledging the impact of decisions on all stakeholders. Sadly, however, in both 2017 and 2018 indexes, teachers overwhelmingly felt that their schools did not proactively monitor their health and well-being.

When placed in the context of objective measures and outcomes, it is not hard to see the many ways in which we can run into problems as teachers. Perception of threat can be something experienced from our own conceptualisation of events and relationships (however true they may be) as well as the actual threats in our environment. The principal issue we have in schools – at every level – is the blockers to the drive-soothe axis. All too often (and probably with good reason), we associate being relaxed and at ease with a lowering of our guard. However, given the degree of natural instability in any school environment – and the many factors outside of our control – life on this threat-drive axis is utterly unsustainable. Indeed, neuroscience even tells us that when we communicate with others with a view to building their self-esteem, we actually activate a different part of the brain compared to when we ask them to reflect on negativity.[22] In essence, in the longer term, it seems that at every level an altogether more sustainable model of education is one that involves us being more reflective and understanding.

The common themes are around celebration, unrelentingly and positively framed high expectations, which call for unwavering academic and moral integrity. How much of this do you see in your schools?

Key points:

- Education is the most human of endeavours and it should be recognised as such: the current framework does not promote this view.

---

22. Simon-Thomas, E. R., Godzik, J., Castle, E., Antonenko, O., Ponz, A., Kogan, A. and Keltner, D. J. (2012) 'An fMRI study of caring vs self-focus during induced compassion and pride', *Social Cognitive and Affective Neuroscience* 7 (6) pp. 635–648.

- Although perhaps it initially came with good intentions, a reliance on outcomes and extrinsic measures is tapping into our threat and drive systems – both collectively and individually.

- The modern educational framework is arguably more open to exploitation and more vulnerable to unscrupulous behaviour, with extrinsic measures and outcomes often used as a justification of this behaviour.

- Schools should be doing much more to support each other, and pitting them against each other in a competitive manner is not an appropriate or effective way of encouraging altruism.

- We need to promote listening and nurturing in our schools as a way of ensuring people can perform at their best. Threat-based strategies are short-sighted and lacking in intellectual and moral credibility and integrity.

Section 3: Compassionate relationships

A. Start with yourself: an individual as part of a much bigger picture
B. Relationships with colleagues
C. Connections with students

Now comes the more practical stuff. Section 2 was more about understanding our context and aimed to provide at least some clarity on the systemic anxiety that plagues much of our education system. This section is about relating to others (and yourself) in your school environment. Hopefully you'll be able to take the ideas and they will be of real use to you in your role. This section is written with the express intent to give you enough proper understanding of the model without wading into too much unnecessary depth; the 'further reading' section at the end of the book will direct you to the right places if that's what you want. The most important relationship we have in life is with ourselves, so I'll start with stuff at the individual level, and then move on to relationships and wider contexts afterwards. Just a quick note – any students or colleague names have been replaced. There is another reason behind this sequence: you cannot be truly compassionate to others until you are compassionate to yourself first and foremost. It's impossible.

A. Start with yourself: an individual as part of a much bigger picture

'Ask not what's inside your head but what your head's inside of.'
William Mace

People – usually barbers and taxi drivers, for some reason – wince when I say I'm a teacher. 'Ooh, you are brave. Hats off to you.' They are referring to the kids, usually. Some of the more discerning will have an idea about the paperwork being ridiculous, with some even commenting on the marking. In any respect, the narrative around the profession is overwhelmingly negative; there is no escaping it. That, I think, plays a large part in the declining mental health of everyone inside it. There's even the insidious narrative from the inside of the cult of the 'hero teacher', with some schools (perhaps unknowingly) celebrating and advocating the sacrifice of work-life balance.

However much we think we are culpable for our depression or anxieties, the first place to start is to see yourself as part of a much bigger picture. You are not your thoughts, nor are you defined by your environment. Does this change things? No. Does a more accurate sense of perspective lead to a heightened feeling of agency and control? Unquestionably.

Please, please do not think I am writing from a perspective of elevated knowledge – I still have plenty of days where the perspective is much harder to reach, and I'm much more exposed to anxiety. I think depression is much like grief: when you lose someone, imagine them as a circle inside of a bigger circle – the bigger circle is your life. As your life grows around it, the person doesn't *shrink*, but your outer circle grows as you move through your life. Some days are lower – naturally – they just aren't like the ones I had before.

There is clear evidence that the way we perceive events manifests in our brains physiologically,[23] and constantly feeling under threat has undeniable links to anxiety and depression through what have been called 'dysfunctional attitudes'.[24] At the heart of the CFT model is dealing with shame and guilt. Threatening cultures lead staff to feel these things about themselves as *individuals* – not just as professionals. With more perspective, we can start to cultivate a more positive self-image.

Unfortunately, the kind of society we live in is very binary: you are either 'good' or you're 'not'. Intrinsic value judgements on people – including our own about ourselves – are mistaken for a sign of intuition and decisiveness. The truth is that there are very few absolutes in life. This is where to start when we think about our own self-image. Missing a deadline or getting it wrong with a student can add to a perceived story we might tell ourselves – one which might make sense and give us clarity, but might actually be profoundly harmful. To perpetuate any sense of an 'OK' self-image, or one that stops us from feeling too low, we can actually become *addicted* to anxiety: we panic about a set of exam results, or a deadline, and when things turn out OK, the hormonal release in our brain and that sense of relief reinforces our need to chase it again. This is more troubling when we think about Section 2 of this book: it's a

---

23. Simon-Thomas, E. R., Godzik, J., Castle, E., Antonenko, O., Ponz, A., Kogan, A. and Keltner, D. J. (2012) 'An fMRI study of caring vs self-focus during induced compassion and pride', *Social Cognitive and Affective Neuroscience* 7 (6) pp. 635–648.
24. Johnson, E. A. and O'Brien, K. A. (2013) 'Self-compassion soothes the savage ego-threat system: effects on negative affect, shame, rumination, and depressive symptoms', *Journal of Social and Clinical Psychology* 32 (9) pp. 939–963.

zero-sum game too – if we're not helping ourselves, our colleagues and students, we're doing them harm. The words of Dame Alison Peacock are especially useful here in terms of the demoralisation that we can experience.

What do you think are the key influences on teacher well-being and mental health?

Alison: Typically the kind of person that wants to become a teacher is someone who is passionate about making a difference, but the job is vast. When that turns into something that feels like *it's* controlling *you* instead of *you* controlling *it*, and if you get to the point where the things that you're being expected to do go beyond the time and capacity that you feel that you have, then it becomes very difficult. You don't want to let the children down, you don't want to let your colleagues and the wider community down – and also the accountability agenda is such that individuals are personally held to account for the performance of others. That's a very difficult place to find yourself when you're worrying about assessment results from other people – there can be all sorts of other factors that can come into play but we're told we're not allowed to make any excuses.

Lost Connections: the vacuum where depression and anxiety thrive

Johann Hari's *Lost Connections*[25] traces human depression back to a range of factors linked by a loss of value, meaning and purpose. One of the cornerstones of the research he came across was that it's not just 'difficulties' (such as really tough ongoing and long-term circumstances) that can cause mental health problems, but also a lack of what researchers called 'stabilisers' in someone's environment (i.e. things that might protect you from negative stuff, such as friends and supportive partners). Too many of the former and too few of the latter is effectively a cocktail for disaster.[26] If you combine long-term difficulties and a lack of

25. Hari, J. (2018) *Lost connections: uncovering the real causes of depression – and the unexpected solutions.* London: Bloomsbury.
26. Brown, G. W. and Harris, T. O. (2011) *Social origins of depression: a study of psychiatric disorder in women.* Abingdon: Routledge.

'stabilisers' in one's personal life, the odds of a mental health problem don't just stack up – they *explode*. As much as anything, this is also about what we perceive to be difficulties and stabilisers too – it's *subjective*. The point here is that given the pace of modern education and its search for meaning and solutions, we are in a somewhat risky business.

In terms of Hari's connections, I've taken the ones here that I feel most obviously link to an educational context. When you consider them, be honest, and be compassionate in terms of their relevance – at this stage, it's about understanding, and being mindful. At the risk of sounding a bit naff, when the truth reveals itself, the sting is taken away. As much as anything, this is about understanding ourselves as humans in a much bigger picture.

Note, these are just questions to reflect upon, and ways of understanding the root causes of how we're feeling about our work – nothing more, nothing less.

1. **Loss of 'meaningful work'.** Focusing on working life, extensive research into the civil service in London found that pay was *not* a major predictor for mental health issues.[27] Rather, the best predictor for mental health troubles was perceived *disempowerment* and a focus on extrinsic measures. As well as this, things like the disconnect between workload, pressure, recognition and lack of balance between efforts and rewards were also major predictors for psychological issues.

   Questions to ask:

   - What positive elements are there to your job? Are you still enjoying those? Why? Why not?

   - How do extrinsic measures such as learning walks, paperwork and evidence-contribution shape the experience of your role?

   - Is your school defined by a core purpose(s) or value(s), or by the systems that govern it? What's given more air time?

---

27. Marmot, M. (2015) *Status syndrome: how your social standing directly affects your health.* London: Bloomsbury.

- Are your days filled with a range of initiatives that are not as rationalised or thoroughly explained as they could be?

- Is student behaviour understood and dealt with in a way that is consistent and supportive to your professional judgement?

- Does the climate in your school feel as if it's OK to get things wrong and learn from them? Or is it a 'one shot and you're done' mentality?

2. **Loss of connection to others.** In numerous studies, perceived loneliness was a major predictor for mental health issues. Think about this: we evolved to be social – it's what gave us our advantage over other species to help us stay close to our groups for protective purposes. When we were away from our group, we had to be more alert – to stop dying, frankly. Research has even found that when we perceive ourselves to be lonely, we experience more sleeplessness.[28] It's the body's way of warning us to seek support. The most dangerous thing about our modern world is that the warning is still valid, but we can nevertheless perceive isolation in the busiest of contexts. Therefore, loneliness leads to a heightened perception of problem seeking. It's even been found that those that feel lonely are better at identifying threats than those that do not feel lonely.[29]

Questions to ask:

- Does your school try to connect its staff and departments? Do meaningful conversations about learning happen? Are they encouraged?

- Is the curriculum linked between subjects? Is there a shared vision of the staff and student experience?

---

28. Preidt, R. (2017) 'Loneliness may lead to sleepless nights', *WebMD* [Online]. Available at: www.bit.ly/2DS4V12 (Accessed 6 Oct 2018).
29. Hawkley, L. C. and Cacioppo, J. T. (2011) 'Perceived social isolation: social threat vigilance and its implications for health' in Decety, J. and Cacioppo, J. T. (eds) *The Oxford handbook of social neuroscience*. Oxford: Oxford University Press, pp. 765–775.

- Is your school trying to connect all stakeholders in meaningful ways – and not just the statutory ones like parents' evenings?

- How and when are leadership communicating with staff?

3. **Loss of meaningful values.** Much in modern society asks us to value material goods. Advertising creates a need for the end user – a void which can only be filled by the purchase of a particular product or service. Not only this, but in both public and private sectors we are valuing those that produce results above all others. In fact, in a study, people placing a disproportionate value on extrinsic measures were more likely to be depressed. Valuing these types of things leads to more poisonous relationships (we only get close to those who can serve us in some way), addiction to short-term goals for reinforcement, and – most crucially – it leads us down a path that ultimately won't give us what we need to live in a contented way. In educational terms, when have a set of exam results ever given us *sustained* pleasure? What are they meant to do – stave off the powers that be for another year by avoiding a poor appraisal or an Ofsted downgrading? The cycle resumes, and so does our addiction to quelling the threat.

Questions to ask:

- Despite what the school says, where do you think it really places value? Would the students agree?

- If you made a pie chart of priorities in your school, how much would you assign to each of the following? Finance, results, student well-being, staff well-being, professional development, anything else.

- How is the annual build up to exams and results feeding and perpetuating anxious patterns?

4. **Loss of status and respect.** Effectively, if our status is threatened, it causes a problem for us; and the more unequal the society, the higher the risk of depression. Things like the *School* documentary are fabulous for raising awareness, but dreadful for morale; and the line of argument in promotional adverts is all about cash and training for free. I don't see status or respect there.

Questions to ask:

- How is the narrative around teaching shaping our own perceptions and experiences of it?
- What narratives are we creating (and sustaining) ourselves?
- How does your school treat its staff – especially the 'weakest'?
- How does your school treat its students – especially the 'weakest'?
- What status and respect is academic rigour given in your school?
- What kind of dialogue is encouraged (or is there room for) in your setting?
- Are good ideas celebrated as a matter of course, or as a 'bolt-on'?

I have to say this: these questions feel like they're from a 'no win, no fee' advert. Anyway, I digress. Of course, like everything we've already talked about, these things also operate on a much wider level. What if schools' work is now defined solely by things that don't speak to *anyone's* intrinsic values? What if school leaders are experiencing such chronic disempowerment that we are growing sick as a collective? What happens to schools in all contexts that don't feel recognised for the work they do? What consequences are there for communities when leaders from schools are isolated from one another, operating as competing silos? What is the impact on teachers when the only real dialogue about the profession emerges when terrible documentaries shed light on the darker experiences of working in schools? I'll not labour this point here, but it's worth giving it some thought. Schools – just like their stakeholders – are bound by a common humanity that is unavoidable, with unavoidably human consequences.

Understanding your personal context

What I love about the CFT model is its basic acknowledgement that we have an unavoidable set of hardware behind everything we think, say or do. As humans with our shiny new neocortex, we've fooled ourselves into thinking the rest of the brain no longer matters; but that's a horrible, horrible misconception. We might not have complete choice and control over our past, our experiences, or our brains, but we can at least be aware of our relationship to the outside world and notice our thoughts about it. The sad fact is that as wonderful a job as teaching is, even in the most wonderful of schools it will throw up any number of deeply frustrating and abominable situations. The key is to recognise the ensuing emotions and not be swallowed up by them. One thing I need to make clear is that in truth, one's individual context is linked with a whole range of factors outside of our control, and some environments are inherently more difficult than others too. So when you read this, remember that your experience in your school is *subjective*, and it'll be unique to others even within your own setting. Some of your threat triggers might be firing because the school isn't a healthy environment for you, or because you may need a little more perspective.

The thing about compassion is that it asks you to be honest with *yourself*. That takes real courage. One of the key attributes to work on is distress-tolerance. Some of the questions you might ask yourself might not yield answers that you'll be very comfortable with. In some cases, teaching may not be for you. If the job is intrinsically making you miserable and it's been the same for an intolerable amount of time, that's OK: you might just need to think of an alternative – and there will be alternatives, no doubt. In other cases, students might irritate you because they remind you of yourself or a difficult experience or memory, or a colleague might be threatening because they might hold up your career – perhaps success takes up a disproportionate percentage of your own self-worth. Perceived failure or negativity is crap, but it's only crap if it's falsely fused with your sense of self-worth or with measures your school deems to be worthwhile. Cruel to be kind? *There is no such thing.* True kindness can only come from a place of nurture and warmth. Anyone that tells you the opposite is a fraud.

In truth, there are so many reasons for teachers to be stressed and unhappy, but if our core purpose and drive are ticking in line with one another, then you can usually get it in perspective. At my lowest, I couldn't. I seriously questioned why I'd gone into teaching. I remember the conversation I had with my parents in Starbucks when I had decided to become a teacher. That bravery and throwing caution to the wind in my first few years – it had all disappeared. I even remember standing in front of a class thinking, 'Why aren't I out there making a multimillion-pound deal with a client or trading derivatives?' (I didn't even know what a derivative was – still don't). I looked at them, then thought, 'You bastard, you can't even get over yourself enough to help the students that need your help. You're pathetic.' So much shame and self-criticism. It's a wonder I ever even made it out of bed in the morning. I'd totally lost my sense of self, and all those things that I drew value from.

Also, in a more mundane everyday sense, it's easy to forget the core purpose of why we go to work given the number of distractions that our environments can throw up – poor behaviour, learning walks, duties, photocopying – the list is endless. The key, as I'll explain, is *noticing* it.

The growth of inner peace

I think we've established that some schools are poorly run, and they feed from anxiety to sustain themselves. If this sounds familiar, then it's probably not a place to be for the long haul. The context discussed in Section 2, I think, is unwittingly forcing us to focus our attentions onto things outside of our influence and our control. Worse still, truly empathetic people are probably more vulnerable because they care so much. Education is probably one of the most 'human' things one can do as a profession; yet most of what drives our current educational system is driven by systems in the brain that are much more reptilian. Can we change this immediately? No. Can we garner a healthier relationship with our thoughts and our contexts? Absolutely.

At one stage for me, the smallest of things would cause waves of anxiety to completely envelop me. I'd spent so much time ignoring the build-up and effect that stress was having on my body – letting it reduce me to that gibbering wreck lying on my parents' couch – that my brain could no longer distinguish between a lion and an email. By the end, an email from someone asking me to set some cover work sent ripples through me so devastating that I had to close my eyes and count to five. It was real. And it was terrifying. Now, I can look back on that version of myself with warmth and empathy. With *compassion*. The compassion that sits in me is so strong that it is my biggest source of hope that I will not find myself in that place again.

As a result, at the time, I used to think, 'Can't we just get rid of the threat part of the brain?' Well, you can take things like diazepam which quell some of the physical sensations linked to threat. But no, you can't just delete threat all together. You need a bit of alertness and adrenaline in some situations anyway. But, as I found, the problems come when thoughts and actions become fuelled by perceived threats. When that happens over a long period of time, it sets off an entirely less productive – and more dangerous – set of thoughts, emotions and feelings. As hinted at before, you can't solve an equation when you're running from a lion, but that is essentially what you are trying to do in this situation. So, although some sense of threat can be helpful, too much is another thing entirely – and boy does our modern context give us reason to fret! There's fairly solid evidence that the act of noticing our feelings is the key to more a more contented life.

At my most vulnerable, I was truly depressed and unable to find any positives to focus on. That was absolutely petrifying. At this point, to some degree, there is a waiting game; but it doesn't mean to say you should stop trying. I started to enjoy coffee more, as I recall. Just focusing on the taste and the intensity of coffee – that was where it kicked off for me. My point is this: however small, find something that brings some element of positivity or reinforcement, and start there. Notice what's good. Eventually, your brain – at whatever level – will start to catch on that it's not being chased by a lion, that threats are often hypothetical, and that that is the best way to confront these things. Just trying to piece together these little victories each day was my antidote because my recognition that I could enjoy and savour *something* gave me the tiniest foundation to build on. So I'd recommend starting small. It might seem pointless, and it might seem trivial, but happiness *does* spread, and it *does* grow.

It was only when I thought 'bugger it' and just focused on a few simple pleasures that the pieces started to fall into place. From that grew other things, and that's when I started to put myself back together. I wrote huge knowledge books for my A level and GCSE classes, and I started to look at a long-term curriculum that would feature things like interleaving and spaced practice – all of those things that we talk about nowadays – and I was thrilled to be part of it. What I loved was the chance to be part of something the wider educational community was discussing, and my drive system began to stir, I guess. I can't explain it, but gradually, my thoughts, feelings and behaviours just began to change. Whether we like it or not, our psychology is quite basic in many ways (says the person writing a book on it…). Just enjoying things made me seek them out more.

I still had days which were appalling. I still do – just less intensely, and less frequently now. Some days, the anxiety finds me more easily; but I am equipped to notice and change something to refocus. Again, the key is to recognise, notice and be compassionate and honest with myself when those days come. Now, when I think of the things that gave me so much emotional pain, I can begin to distance myself from the narrative of myself as unworthy, and I hold my values closer. That reminds me of what's important. As the opening of the book hopefully explained, our brains are wired for anxiety and worry – and we can't help it. There is no doubt at all that beginning to notice our thoughts, emotions, feelings and behaviours allows us to defuse the negativity and gain that all important perspective (recall that Section 1 addressed the need to create space between us and our difficult thoughts or feelings). At the same time, uncertainty and discomfort are a reality of life: we do need to be aware of situations and developments in the future, but we just need to be mindful of the line between the present and conjecturing too far unnecessarily.

The merry-go-round we need to jump off: thoughts, emotions, feelings and behaviour

What pretty much all successful psychological models have in common is a thorough and proper understanding of our thought processes. The complexity of the brain and our environment give rise to all kinds of thoughts; and whilst we can't stop it, we can understand the nature of a trigger – to a thought, to a feeling, to a physical sensation (which, by the way, usually makes us feel the initial thought more intensely). It's one of the oldest psychological models; we can't stop it, really, but we can make it less intense. So, for sake of illustration (and remember these occur in no particular order):

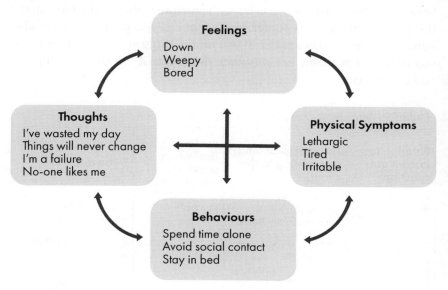

Diagram from Moodjuice,[30] based on Padesky and Mooney, 1990.

Note here that emotions are more primal, whereas feelings are a way of making sense of the emotion. Debbie Hampton puts it best:

> Feelings are sparked by emotions and coloured by the thoughts, memories, and images that have become subconsciously linked with that particular emotion for you ... While individual emotions are temporary, the feelings they evoke may persist and grow over a lifetime. Because emotions cause subconscious feelings which in turn initiate emotions and so on, your life can become a never-ending cycle of painful and confusing emotions which produce negative feelings which cause more negative emotions without you ever really knowing why.[31]

---

30. Diagram found at www.bit.ly/2HQr1Fg
31. Hampton, D. (2015) 'What's the difference between feelings and emotions?', *The Best Brain Possible* [blog]. Available at: www.bit.ly/2MROuox (Accessed 31

We've every right to have all of these emotions, thoughts and feelings, but in noticing them, we can choose any of the *behaviours* (see the table below). But this is where it gets tricky: sometimes, it's about choosing the thing which might feel counterintuitive in order to get the best possible outcome. The bad news is that if you do the thing your gut instinct tells you to, it will probably just reinforce the negativity in the cycle for you and the student.

Event: Student ignores me and doesn't complete homework			
Emotion (an instant gut reaction)	Thought (planning/responding to the event)	Feeling (based on previous experiences)	Behaviour
Anger	'This is pointless – why waste my time?' 'What is wrong with this child!' 'OK, what can I change to make this better?' 'Can I even change this?'	Frustration	Choice 1: Say 'OK, let's talk after' Choice 2:Say 'Why do I bother?' Choice 3: Say 'Same again, is it? That's to be expected, isn't it?' Choice 4: Say 'Right, I'm going to call home'

The key to understanding this is that the mind and body are somehow divorced and unlinked. 'I think therefore I am?' Nonsense. I *am* because I've got a bloody massive knot in my tummy and a ten-tonne weight on my chest when I wake up every morning! Our bodies can tell us things we are not even consciously aware of. I honestly believe this misunderstanding is where a lot of mental illness comes from.

As the table above shows, whatever situation we find ourselves in, it can lead to an emotion, a thought, a feeling or a behaviour. In truth you can hop on this merry-go-round at any point, and off you go. There's nothing

Mar 2018).

intrinsic about thoughts and worries: they are one part of a big cycle that is self-reinforcing. *Noticing* is the key – and when you begin to *notice*, you'll see that your brain takes you off into all kinds of funny places.

When you are anxious, ask yourself the following:

- Was there a trigger that began the worry?
- What are you saying to yourself?
- If you are criticising yourself, and this critical voice could speak to you, what would it sound like? What tone of voice would be it using?
- Do you truly believe what you're saying? What is grounded in fact? What is grounded in perception?
- What are the physical sensations that you're experiencing alongside this?
- What function is the anxiety or worry serving? Remember the difference between awareness and something that becomes stifling.

It's probably worth hanging on that last bullet point for a moment. At my worst, things that initially used to fire and drive me turned into crippling anxiety-provoking thoughts. I'm an A level teacher, and used to revel in my confidence with teaching the course, but I suddenly began to focus on all those things that the students might not know, and the possibilities of exam questions that might reveal my weaknesses as a teacher. The textbook began to feel like an insurmountable challenge – it actually felt *heavier* in my hand. Sure, a little bit of awareness and reflection is useful, but the amount it began to affect me was counterproductive. I was chatting to someone in business the other day who said that their worry and fear of failure drove their success: they had to carry out due diligence on complex contracts and make sure things went well in the purchase of companies. I'd wager that poring through contracts and checking details is simply not possible if your brain is threat-addled. I'd also wager that there was more than a bit of drive going on for this person to have enjoyed the success they had over that period of time. Of course, I could be wrong. But one thing I am not wrong about is the long-term implications of living life on that threat-drive axis. In the same way, hard work in teaching is inevitable, but we need to reflect on whether hacking through an extra pile of books is any good for us or the students in proportion to the time we might spend on it. It's also important to notice how we're feeling when we sit down to mark: what's driving us to mark? Is it curiosity? Or is it fear of being found, judged and input as a 'red' teacher?

Seeing thoughts for what they are

I don't find tonnes of specific – and possibly unrelatable – examples all that helpful; but for sake of illustration, one could be useful here in terms of the process. The example I'll use is the language around performance management. I appreciate the glaring issue with seeing things in the way this table does as it totally ignores the variability of schools and their approach to 'performance management'; but the point is to see how our environment can spark our reactions:

Event: 'We'll start the first round of lesson observations next week. You'll be seen with 10X2' (who happen to be my nightmare class...)			
Emotion	**Thought**	**Feeling**	**Behaviour**
Fear – threatened and concerned about the future	1. 'Oh no – they'll be a nightmare. That's my performance management down the drain'	Panic and anxiety – tenseness in chest and stomach	Over resourcing/ over-detailed lesson plan/ high-stakes conversations with students/ avoidance
Anger – I hate this place!	2. 'This is a pile of crap – more evidence that this school doesn't know how to assess learning'	Frustration – tense/ hopelessness/ exasperation	No real action taken to make it a positive experience
Determination – how can I draw a positive from this?	3. 'OK, not ideal, but there are plenty of positive aspects for someone to see'	Energy and drive	Thinking through the lesson as part of a bigger picture – knowing that this will demonstrate true learning

It's worth noting that the distinction between emotions and feelings isn't always obvious. The word 'round' when talking about a set of lesson observations also has connotations of being treated like a number, as if leadership are herding sheep. Nothing personal. Nothing in the way of individuality. No, this is not about political correctness; this is about being aware of how language can play into already anxious minds. By the way, what an absolutely abhorrent term – 'performance': it's surface level, and I seriously doubt that you can punitively 'manage' someone to perform better in the way that the word suggests. In some cases, such is the path that some in schools have trodden: threat becomes the sole currency that they deal in (sometimes masked as 'drive').

Looking at the table, then, and thinking about the notion of 'toxic schools', we can really see the spread of poor mental health in such settings. Just imagine extrapolating this table out into an entire staff or student body. Terrifying. This table might look overly simple. And of course, everyone's reactions to this type of thing will be different. But the key is to begin to separate our thoughts from the emotions, behaviours and feelings that follow. Of course, it doesn't take a genius to separate the helpful sequences from the unhelpful sequences above. Part of being self-compassionate is about accepting that you might feel frustration about the process, but you don't have to choose the behaviour that follows in that row: you can still do the thing that leads to a positive outcome as much as is possible. So, you feel it's futile? I'd say, however hard it might feel, you could always try and pick something to focus on in the lesson. Ask whoever is coming in to look at that *with* you and be proactive – then you'll be able to reflect on your choices with warmth and kindness. Part of being self-compassionate is making these choices, which may help us to realise we need to leave our environments. This is about self-awareness and truth.

There may well be all kinds of narratives getting in the way of you doing this; but where possible, I'd say investing hope and passion into something will result in better mental well-being. It's also helpful to think about the kind of internal trains of thought you might be having around this as well. These sequences can reinforce all kinds of stories we tell ourselves, resulting in self-fulfilling prophecies:

- 'I hate observations'
- 'I've never been good at being watched'
- 'That's always a bad lesson'
- 'I don't like visitors in my classroom'
- 'X will know I'm being observed and will be a nightmare on purpose'
- 'The students will not play ball on the day'

Inevitably, thoughts, feelings, and narratives are interconnected. Being self-compassionate is about understanding this. The truth is, we come into this world with our magnificent (albeit deeply flawed) brains, and to acclimatise ourselves emotionally, socially and culturally, we tell ourselves all kinds of things which might make sense in the short term and enable us to understand our situations, but in the longer term are actually very unhelpful.

Broadening this out, I suppose it might be useful to reframe the above sequence like this:

1. **Event:** 'We'll start the first round of lesson observations next week. You'll be seen with 10X2' (who happen to be my nightmare class...)

2. **Notice:** What's my impulse? What's my gut telling me? What's that based on? What experiences/narratives/perceptions am I basing this on?

3. **Plan:** What's the most productive thing I can do now? Plan? Just leave it for now (if it's weeks/months away) and be aware of it – let it sit but keep it in mind? Take a quick look at the books to calibrate where they are?

There's fairly strong evidence to suggest that this type of sequence will, to some extent, retrain your brain to experience difficulties more effectively. Other shorter-term measures (longer-term if you continue to practise, of course) that people often find useful include:

- **A self-care charter.** Make a list of, say, three things you can commit to each week (don't necessarily beat yourself up if you can't achieve them!). Give yourself space and value yourself enough to do these things. It might be going to the gym, making a decent dinner, or listening to an audiobook.

- **Thought-trackers.** This can be for negative and/or positive things you notice about your thoughts and what they might be saying about you.

- **Visualisation.** This might sound odd, but it works for loads of people. Pick a place/moment/food/anything that brings you pleasure, and really try to visualise it or experience that pleasure in your mind's eye. It's not a *Harry Potter* Pensieve-type scenario; it's more about the mental images – whatever they are – being brought to mind. Again, it's about the most basic thing of experiencing something positive in your mind, and letting your mind and body know it's OK.

- **The 4-7-8 breathing method.** A tried-and-tested method which can help your mind back to 'neutral'. Simply breathe in for four seconds, pause for seven, and then breathe out through your mouth for eight seconds. If those timings don't work for you, just adjust them. There are also plenty of breathing apps for smartphones which can guide you through to calming your mind – I'd thoroughly recommend them. I read recently that people often feel anxious because they forget to breathe out. It seems odd, but I like the fact that when I breathe out in a more pronounced way through my mouth, I feel my chest ease and relax.

As much as possible, it's about flipping narratives on themselves, and about understanding the connection between emotions and behaviour. That is *much* easier said than done, but it is important. Once we can start to notice our anger and frustration in a situation, it can begin to dissipate or de-intensify. I suppose, then, if we are having uncomfortable thoughts, we could ask the following questions:

- What's the worst thing that can happen?
- Underneath, what does this thought or feeling tell me about my values? At core, what am I worried about? Is it a self-perception thing? Is it the way others might perceive me?
- Is the uncomfortable thought feeding into some kind of negative narrative about myself?
- Is this thought or feeling linked with something similar in my past? Where might the connection come from?

It's important to try to make time for this type of thing during the day too. Even if you don't feel it's possible, it's *always* possible. Even becoming mindful of your thoughts, emotions and feelings in any given situation can be transformative – I promise. To an extent, we need to make space where we can to notice our thoughts and feelings. Think of it this way: if you've ever tried out one of those virtual reality headsets, it's amazing how you can attune yourself to actually being in the world you are looking at – but it's not real. The ability to take the glasses off – and always know you can – is empowering. We just need to remember to. Sometimes, it's also a case of noticing your emotions and feelings as you experience them as well. Standing 'outside' is an important part of this.

Acute anxiety and stress

It's worth reflecting on those times when things can feel unbearable. As I've alluded to, the beauty of our brain is in the imagination – the hypothesising, planning and fantasising. We can have goals, ideas, plans and all those kinds of things, and lots of those can be healthy. But if they begin to define you, then you're living in a hypothetical world that doesn't *really* exist. Imagine a scenario of Ofsted, an observation, a troubling class. Your rumination can be paralysing, but it won't do you any good: it will make you *less* able to come up with strategies to deal with it.

In the *really* short term, I'd recommend 'soothing rhythm breathing'. If you search this online, there are a number of free clips that will guide you through it. All it does is physically let your mind know that you are fundamentally safe, and that the threats you are perceiving and ruminating on are hypothetical, and not really life-threatening, which is what the physiological response is designed to deal with. To be blunt, when your heart rate is up, and your breathing is rapid, it's your body's way of sending in the cavalry – even if it's not really needed.

If you're finding things difficult to the point where life is overly uncomfortable, then with the right time and space, I'd start by reflecting on something that brings you a degree of happiness – it can be inside or outside of work – and then build on that. Do things that bring positivity and happiness. Relish that life can still bring you lots of happiness. Ask yourself:

- What one thing have I always enjoyed doing (in either work or personal life)?
- Is there someone who makes me smile or who helps me to feel safe?
- Is there something I can do that I'm confident will work in a lesson?
- What's coming up over the next few weeks that I can look forward to?

Reflecting on these things and taking them to a line manager/colleague/ someone who can affect change can be really productive and empowering. It may seem counterintuitive when you may want to run and hide, but proactivity can be really useful. The words of Dame Alison Peacock here are useful should you find yourself in a truly intolerable situation.

What would you say in the short term to colleagues in really difficult environments?

Alison: There will be other colleagues in your team even if they're not in your department. There will be other colleagues who are like-minded and are the kind of people that build you up as opposed to knock things down. Seek those people out when you need people to align with. Also, try to make sure that every day you allow yourself to think about something that has gone well – remember the exchange you had with a youngster who chose to come and speak to you or somebody who achieved something more than they thought they were going to be able to. Remember also that the children and young people in the school where you work need you; and if you are someone who is finding it difficult because the culture feels very harsh then chances are you will be the kind of teacher that young people will really value because they will sense in you that you're someone who cares about them.

Toxic vs tough environments

'Toxic' is an emotive term. To some extent, it needs contextualising: no one sets out to create a toxic school. But the experience of the people in them is unmistakable. The sad truth is that there do exist some environments whereby your threat system will rightly be firing – because it's trying to protect you. If you are feeling like that, and you've exhausted all possibilities, the obvious thing is to find somewhere else.

If there is a constant flow of unreasonable demands, and a real lack of a clearly communicated focus, vision or strategy to underpin the everyday workings of the school, then I'd suggest things are untenable. And, sadly, I think it will only take enough leaving the profession to help everyone realise that this is too all too commonplace.

I would make a slight distinction between a 'toxic' environment and a 'tough' one, though. And as you know, schools *are* tough. What I mean by this is that we need to remember the size of organisations that schools are, and someone will be responsible for the systems in place to make sure things run smoothly. So, we might get senior leaders or pastoral staff walking around at duty points to check that staff are there. We might have really strict data deadlines that result in a 'conversation' if you miss them. We might have sickness meetings when we return to work following a day of lying in bed with a fever. All of these things can induce anxiety, but they are, to a large extent, a necessity of any big organisation. Those extrinsic checking mechanisms are just a safety measure, and it's important that they are held in the right perspective. If they become defining for a school or its teachers, then the dialogue and the agenda has moved into a different sphere. Even in the wonderful book *Drive*, Pink acknowledges that extrinsic systems are only really effective for more mundane stuff – like arriving at a duty point on time.

Where the problem lies in schools is either if they are using extrinsic systems for rather more unscrupulous behaviours and targeting individuals, or if systems are defining the softer side of things – the more complex stuff. It's all very well having a checklist for a learning walk for the sake of brevity and clarity, but if the conversations that follow aren't transparent and two way, then we ought to question what the point of them is anyway – we'd just be valuing what we measure as a poor substitute for a credible conversation.

It's important as an individual to think about where your school is positioned amongst all of this. That matters, because there is a distinction between how you are feeling and whether the school is perhaps operating in an unhealthy way:

- Are systems clear and communicated in advance?
- Is there enough in place to support everyone to do what they need?

- When conversations take place that may have difficult aspects, are they two-way, meaningful and fair?

It's important to answer these questions with total honesty – *compassionately*. I'd suggest if the answer to these questions is 'no' then something in your school needs to change. No one thinks for a second that life in schools is easy – we sign up for the hard work. But in the context of punitive threats and an over-reliance on systems, there is no long-term future for that type of school.

Here would be a wonderful time to bring in Jamie Thom's thoughts on this topic. Again, his thoughts on slowing down and being more mindful seemed to sit extremely well with the notion of compassion. (At one point I joked with him that we should write a 'Slowly Compassionate' book – poor Jamie!) Before moving onto relationships and staying with us as an individual, his thoughts are worth considering.

What aspects of 'slow teaching' link most closely with mental health?

Jamie: I think in teaching one of the things that drives people away is the relentless pace and the fact that expectations of people – particularly in the first few years – are really intensive, and a lot of the time it's all just unrealistic. It's also damaging for people and their motivation and their desire to do well. 'Slow teaching' isn't about sloth-like teaching, but about being more reflective on *how* you spend your time in school. One of the problems with leaders is that they don't reflect on the demands they're putting on teachers. There's that sense that if teachers are working 60, 70, 80 hours a week, then that's something to be *celebrated* rather than something to be horrified about, putting people who are starting out in the profession under that degree of pressure. The 'slow teaching' concept would suggest that everybody in the whole school is more reflective about how time is being used, and everybody's thinking about it through the lens of what expectation is being placed on the person that they're asking things of – that in turn there's a calmer culture. In some schools there's not that sense of being calm and doing things for the right reason. There's a conveyor belt of expectation that doesn't ultimately lead to improved outcomes or an improved experience for everyone involved.

Do you think it is the system or the leaders that are set up to fail?

Jamie: Ultimately it's the fear factor: people go through Ofsted reports and expectations like they are gospel. Every single thing they say is then implemented with the staff body. If Ofsted says 'triple marking' then that's filtered down. There have been some really positive changes that have happened in the last few years, but things like data – this obsession with data – just frustrates teachers. You find that you're constantly having conversations about data rather than about how young people are learning in your classes. And your performance management is based entirely on data, so the whole conversation loses that sense of motivation. I also think there are some really brave leaders in schools and they're saying, 'We will do what's right for our school community and our school body that will ultimately be the best for our teachers and our students.' So there needs to be more of that. There needs to be more of a sense that schools can take ownership.

How would you recommend managing your workload as an individual teacher then?

Jamie: The first thing is that well-being has got to be deeply personal to the individual. People talk about yoga or mindfulness, but every teacher is different and every teacher works in a different way. The first way of managing your workload is being comfortable in how you work as an individual. If you're someone who likes to work in the morning and get in early, do that and leave early for example. It's about working out your own mechanisms of how to flourish and be successful. The temptation with teaching is that it is the kind of job where you could just go 100% for seven days a week. For a perfectionist it can sometimes be the worst job in the world because you think you've never got to the place you want to be in. So that's the other part to consider: the danger that you have to be aware of is your perfectionist drive, other people, and how they influence how you work.

I also think that one of the things we focus on too much is the short term rather than the long term, so trainees are encouraged to plan individual lessons and to spend hours poring over PowerPoints and the individual learning experience. We need to be more strategic in our teaching and in our classroom, and that will help manage our workload. There needs to be so much more in terms of the coaching we can do to help teachers manage. Whenever people are anxious and stressed, their filter closes in and they can only think within individual lessons and spaces. We should be sufficiently confident as a profession to respect teachers enough to say that learning walks and books and all that sort stuff are not really going to help a more experienced teacher to improve. It's likely to frustrate them more than anything else.

I love Jamie's ideas about autonomy and reclamation of what is important. Integrity is vital at every level. This, of course, starts at the top; but if we can be mindful, compassionate and – yes – *slow*, we can surely gain that perspective and inner sense of calm to settle our minds and help us make the right calls for ourselves, our colleagues and our students. (More on this in Section 4.)

B. Relationships with colleagues

'We are human BEings not human DOings.'
John Bradshaw

Of course, the diversity and range of relationships we have in our settings is enormous. I won't even attempt to address all of these here; however, I think it's worth noting – as Mary Myatt said to me – that we see everyone as 'people first'. By this, I mean recognising their *humanity*. A knowing smile, a nod, an 'OK?' to anyone and everyone in a school environment goes a long way and can't be underestimated.

In terms of relationships, I'm going to start with some school-wide notions of compassion, and then move into the notion of feedback – both giving and receiving. Parts will be of more direct relevance to some than others, but I think relationships are universal, and so are the considerations within the next few pages.

Staff culture and compassion-focused staff bodies

In many ways, this is probably the trickiest aspect of working in schools. Teaching is a profession unlike any other: you are effectively baring a best version of yourself to young people for hours on end each day, and it is utterly relentless. The staff-to-student ratios, lack of non-contact time and so forth naturally breeds an overly hectic work environment. Beyond the classroom, there's also a sense that we're all so rushed off our feet that it's difficult to form those compassionate relationships that really see us through. It's quite sad as well to see the death of the staff room in many places now – places to decompress and have that space to be a more relaxed version of ourselves.

It's already been mentioned that having and sustaining an impact are two different skill sets. I think it's the same when it comes to being compassionate. Being compassionate isn't an isolated thing: it's about *recognising* the difficulties of others in *every* situation. I'm shocking for it. Sometimes I'll stand behind some poor soul in the photocopying queue five minutes before my lesson feeling irritated that they (and not the machine!) can't go any quicker. Or I'll be apoplectic that there's no water in the kettle again and the nearest tap is a 50-yard walk down the corridor. Apart from being more organised, and bothering to do something nice and fill the kettle up myself for once, taking the time to recognise these things isn't only going to benefit others: CFT reminds us that it has real benefits within our own minds too.

In truth, there is a balance between noticing more helpful behaviours, and whether or not we are in the right place to always do something about it. I might be stood in that photocopying queue because my car broke down, or I stopped a fight downstairs, or I might have just left it until the last minute. Either way, noticing the feeling and keeping in mind the three-part brain system is important. I'm annoyed at the person in front not because I hate them, but because of my own anxieties – nothing more, nothing less. Remember, at its heart, compassion is about having a sensitivity to others' suffering as well, and being compelled to alleviate it. This isn't about ignoring your own issues to help others all of the time, but it is about being mindful of what someone else is going through. That nightmare class you taught last year? Yep, someone has them this year, and they might be struggling with them too. That class that were a bit spicy last year but you got on well with? Yep, someone has them now, but they're a nightmare for them. That colleague who you've not seen all week because they've been rushing around or been off? A nod, a check, or simply a look can make a huge difference. Of course, the benefits of being attuned to this are massive for your own engagement with the world, and for your own sense of soothe.

Inhibitors: blockers to compassion

Importantly, there are also what we call inhibitors of being compassionate – things that get in the way. Threat and drive gets things done; they can be seen as indicators of competence and decisiveness. What is really dangerous, however, is when this is underpinned by poor proxies of credibility or integrity, giving some in their minds carte blanche to behave as they wish. By the way, I include myself in this to a certain point: at my lowest, I stopped proactively advocating and fighting for my own team, and I should have done more.

Looking at ourselves, I'd imagine it's quite difficult to feel compassion for people we don't like, don't identify with, or don't have a prior relationship with. On the flipside, if your best buddy has been off for a couple of days, I bet you'd be less inclined to think that they're just sacking it off sitting at home in their PJs watching Netflix. Even if you did think that, perhaps you'd be more likely to understand *why*. We identify and have compassion more easily for those who have evoked similar feelings in us.

As well as this, Rutger Bregman's 'mental bandwidth' is useful here. It's harder to have the energy to be compassionate when you're knackered/stressed yourself, and when you basically feel like you have less time for the person you might be engaging with. That's where *noticing* comes in: in other words, recognising your own threats that might be inhibiting you from being a human being first and foremost. A useful exploration here is to visualise (like before) your feelings and emotions for someone you love – imagine them being upset and your response. Then do it with someone you have no real connection with. Then with someone you have a bit of a dislike for. Again, the key here is the mindful noticing of differences in your gut reactions. Although schools are supposed to fundamentally be the most human of institutions, we so often forget the common humanity we all share. In many ways, the context is actually pulling us apart so we can less easily see and feel the humanity we share. The key to this is that we are non-judgemental in our thoughts – which can be really, really tricky.

We might have a line manager or a colleague that evokes a sense of threat in us. I'd say step one is to notice it, and think about *why*. Is it something about their unpredictability? Is it their modus operandi? Is it that they've made you feel something about yourself that you're not entirely comfortable with? The other side of this coin, of course, is that the way people choose to behave can also be covering up any number of their own feelings: anger and aggression can be a means of concealing discomfort or insecurity; decisiveness can be a means of concealing uncertainty; and so it goes on. Does reflecting on these things change anything? Probably not, but I would say this was the most transformative element of the model for me; I could see the people who were threatening me and start to unpick their points of departure. They weren't powerful overlords who wanted to destroy me; they had bosses themselves – bosses who were kicking their backsides with their own threat-addled minds. Dismissing people as evil is too simplistic (not to mention unhelpful).

Looking elsewhere, though, one thing I *love* about schools is that there are untapped alleyways of friendship all over the place. You begin working in your department and get settled with your own group. But as you get more established, you don't realise that there's a chemistry teacher down the corridor with a season ticket at your favourite football club, or that the teaching assistant (remember those?) who's been supporting little Amy for the last four weeks also loves that TV series you've been binging on (*Gotham*, since you asked). I think it's really important to see people as people first and foremost – schools are overwhelmingly filled with decent, caring and often hilarious people.

However (and as alluded to before) what we are dealing with in teaching at the moment are some fairly fundamental and systemic blockers to compassion – I would even say to the extent that we are suspicious of those who want to be kind to us. We're time-poor. We're resource-poor. We are under outrageous pressure. Who has time to be *nice*?

'What's that? Hannah's done tray bakes again and left them in the office? Bloody do-gooder.'

'Oh yeah, there Colin goes again, volunteering to step in and do a duty. Bloody brown noser on the whole-school email.'

There's no doubt at all that there might be some elements of truth to these narratives – but my point is that there is no need to see this in an entirely threat-focused way. Maybe Colin is ambitious; why should that be derided? Or maybe he feels like he has something to prove to others, so is actually a little bit unhappy? There are endless possibilities, and we needn't always take the most reductionist and negative one. Perhaps more importantly for us, always seeing the worst in people is no good for the way we see ourselves either. Maybe viewing Colin as ambitious is revealing something about our own insecurity? Poor Colin – he only volunteered to cover a duty.

From DOing to BEing: buzzwords and bullshit

What really, really, irks me about buzzwords in schools is the lack of *values* behind them. In lots of environments, there's an unwitting line of thought that 'professional challenge' and 'getting out of our comfort zone' is all about being a 'healthy growth mindset environment'. Saying it doesn't make it so, as they say.

A colleague of mine once told me that their headteacher decided that their school would become a 'growth mindset school'. As a result, every classroom would need some sort of growth mindset display on the walls. To get something working it needed to be 'in everyone's faces – all of the time'. In order to ensure this was done effectively, the leadership team would then be conducting learning walks of every room in the school to check that this had been done. (And in case you're wondering, the leadership team were not being ironic when they added the bit about learning walks.) If you want to check that the displays have been completed as one indication of buy-in and understanding, there is no need to announce and formalise it; just follow it up with a sensible conversation afterwards. Rather, though, they were so utterly overtaken by what growth mindset would *look* like that they didn't have time to think about what it should *feel* like. My point is this: if you aren't living out those values, don't waste your time proclaiming that you are.

A useful way of drawing this out is to consider an inspirational leader or colleague you've worked with at some stage. Why were they successful? I'd bet it was because they inspired, because they were consistent, and because they weren't defined by fear, but by courage, warmth and empathy. They didn't accept people just sacking it off; they want the best for their teams and their students; their values and their execution are in sync; and their altruism was reciprocated through hard work and authenticity – not fear and avoidance of judgement. These things are *infectious*, and they are *enduring*.

Whether we like it or not, as professionals in schools, we exist in a range of contexts, all of which shape our threat, drive and soothe systems every time we draw breath. That doesn't mean we shouldn't have meaningful professional challenge or ask difficult questions, but these things won't be received or heard unless we take a person's context into account. These aren't excuses; they're environmental considerations that are inextricably linked to how we are feeling at any given time. I'd argue that at whatever level, simply noticing your emotional and physical feelings is vital to be able to have a meaningful interaction with anybody. Be professional? Yes. Shut off from recognising one's own humanity and the humanity of others? No way. Rather, I think we should at least acknowledge the realities that surround ourselves and our colleagues every day:

- **Immediate**: Events during the day – photocopier exploding/ whiteboard malfunctioning/class difficulty in certain periods of a day. (I'm literally listing things as I think of them.)
- **Personal**: Pets/neighbours/family/friends – relationships and illness
- **Professional** (school): Feelings about role/position within school/ support/autonomy
- **Professional** (wider): Narrative around school/profession

Receiving feedback

Because learning is open ended, instantaneous yet long-term, there will always be things you can improve in a lesson, whether you teach 1 or 30 lessons a week. Again, it is harder for some than others to receive feedback for any number of reasons. For me, it almost entirely depends on my relationship with the person giving it to me. Do I trust them? Do they rate me? What angle are they coming from? How valid is their feedback in my mind? How valid is their feedback in reality? There's a personal and wider context to feedback, whatever anyone says, and it's important to recognise this rather than being swept up in threat-focused narratives and responses.

Apart from anything else, given that so much of teaching in our present context is bound up in individuality, we are naturally very bound up within ourselves, I think. The result? Irrespective of our school environment, being told that we need to do something additional, extra, or even less of something can be really difficult to hear.

Again, the mechanisms are actually remarkably similar to the previous section. Let's say you've received some indifferent lesson feedback – I know I have in my time. I'm a bit precious about my teaching: I try to present that I am relaxed about having people in, and I am secure in my own pedagogy, but deep down there is a level of discomfort about being watched in any kind of formal way. There needs to be a huge amount of respect and awareness for any colleague who is on the receiving end of feedback (as I'll discuss below), but this is about how we might react to feedback and why. I think it's important to recognise what we are bringing into the room with us, so to speak, when we receive any kind of feedback. Only when we are honest enough about this can we really receive feedback in a meaningful way. I've always found it useful to make myself aware and notice my own thoughts prior to receiving feedback. Let's imagine this in a three-step scenario: before, during and after receiving feedback. Again, this is subjective and to some extent depends on the person giving the feedback, but we can exert control and shape our own experience to a large degree.

Before: How do I feel the lesson went? What's my emotion? How is it connecting to physical sensations I might be experiencing? What narratives about my teaching or my students is this linking with? This is where compassion is useful, but also breathing and visualisation in order to bring the idea of soothe to the forefront of our minds if that's what is needed.

During: Irrespective of the situation, it's vital that we hear feedback about our performance with real kindness about ourselves. Opinions and questions are fine as long as they tap into a genuine sense that we want to improve; but tapping into narratives and harsh criticisms of ourselves is another thing altogether. For example:

Something an observer might say-	Unhelpful/unkind/harsh narratives and judgements	Compassionate responses
How do you feel it went?	• They want me to admit it was crap • The same things were poor – and it's linked to my poor abilities • I felt it was OK, but you obviously didn't • This is another one in a long line of crappy reflections	• Irrespective of the overall feel, there's an opportunity to reflect on some positives • The lesson is a snapshot, and one moment in time – it is not intrinsically linked to my abilities • I felt confident in lots of aspects of the lesson such as _____ but would like to reflect more on _____
I liked it when you...	• Oh god, that's the 'nice part'. Overall it was still rubbish. They always have to find something nice to say	• Yes, I understand why that would have been seen as a positive: can I use it again or extend it in some way? • What were the useful elements here? What made it effective and how can I do more of it?
Some of the students were unsure at that point	• I planned poorly – I wasn't aware of that • No, it was fine – they'd have got there in the end • Yeah, but they're a nightmare and they're never going to get it right	• It'd be useful if I could make it explicit for everyone to alleviate any of my own uncertainty about this • Cleaning up uncertainty when I haven't seen it will make for a much more productive lesson environment • Some students will definitely struggle more than others, and it'll be useful to catch as many as possible so they don't have an excuse to avoid and opt out

Something an observer might say-	Unhelpful/unkind/harsh narratives and judgements	Compassionate responses
I'd be concerned if Ofsted were in	• They're coming for me and I'm going to be found out • This is more evidence to someone that I'm useless and struggling	• Ofsted is a separate entity, and not really linked to this discussion – I'm going to focus on steering my own improvement • Indeed, this is the *observer's* concern, not mine. It's a shame they're feeling that but my driver is for my students and me

Again, compassion doesn't mean making excuses and dismissing difficulty: it's the opposite. Ultimately, our values are linked with progress and relationships, and being open and receptive to improving things is our responsibility.

As well as a tricky brain, we have a tricky *context* in schools, as so much of what we experience is defined by those around us. Some of you may recognise the bottom row from the BBC Two documentary School. In it, the observer was rather negative to the teacher; it certainly didn't seem as if the teacher left the room with any sense of soothe or drive in terms of improving things. Rather, the observer simply transferred their own anxieties about inspection onto them. It was difficult to feel anything but distaste for the observer, and anything but sympathy for the teacher. Later on, however, the difficulties the observer experienced in their wider role were explored. Knowing about these difficulties doesn't change the invalidity of the point about Ofsted, nor does it excuse the negative way that the feedback was handled, but it does help us to understand others' points of departure and struggles. No one has it 'easy'. Just noticing and being aware of another's problems defuses some of the tension around our relationships. Of course, when we feel threatened, it's really tough to feel compassion for those that are threatening us – but this is precisely the point. Recognising all of our common humanity will ease that tension, and 'lowering one's guard' needn't mean being taken for a fool. The issue is that, given that performance, careers and pay are linked to these situations, there are often many inhibitors of feeling compassion for one another.

I am prone to being overly emotional and catastrophising, so I know as much as anyone how difficult these situations can be. But I do now genuinely believe that compassion is the way to deal with them. And it does mean starting with yourself. Start by acknowledging your own anxieties and pain, and where they come from. Recognising it in someone else is not about letting your defences down or making yourself vulnerable – you are only vulnerable when you live in a world clouded by negativity and anxiety. If we think about it, we might find ourselves living in a threat-fuelled anxiety-ridden bubble. It might just work in the short term at some level; you might feel like it's making you more aware and able to anticipate things that will go wrong. But that, if you recall, is probably what has gone wrong at every level of educational governance – especially in recent times.

After: This book isn't a list of self-help activities: it's about asking you to unpick and notice your thoughts and experiences. As I've mentioned, it's important to separate out your thoughts, emotions, feelings and behaviours – *they are not the same thing*. Collectively, they become narratives, as the tables above illustrate at least to some level. The important thing is that we recognise these aspects of our experience, and do something useful with them. So, if we're feeling anxious, stressed, upset or maybe even buoyed about something that's happened in our day, then we need to notice it. If I'm anxious, I find it's helpful to have a chat to someone who empathises and has a warmth for you. This is good for getting your soothe system back online. However, if my predominant feeling is of adrenaline or stress, I've found going to the gym or getting out of the environment is the most useful thing. Do something entirely unrelated to work if you can; remove yourself from the context. It's important to remember that some of these things might feel counterintuitive – you might want to confront and address it instantly (perhaps even impulsively – I'm shocking for that), but perspective is gained by stepping away. Once you're in a place to think more constructively, you'll find responding to feedback much easier. One key here is to try to recognise your own response to feedback. Might you want to push back and disagree? Is it for logistical and rational reasons, or because maybe it makes you feel a bit uncomfortable? Again, it's worth bringing you back to the notion of a *toxic* environment or a *tough* environment – each of which is relative.

Giving feedback

Taking this back to threat, drive and soothe, let's start from the assumption that, for the majority of people, being observed is a tough thing. Hearing feedback about something you've probably put your heart and soul into is tough: 'This is the very best version I can offer – if there's something up with it, then there's something up with *me*.' This can only be magnified depending on the wider school environment (e.g. the growth mindset story above). I spoke to Mary Myatt about this – her work seemed to fit perfectly onto this model.

Do you have any advice for teachers in schools that aren't conducive to positive mental health?

Mary: There are some places that are absolutely *toxic*. There's no question about that and in those contexts people need to get out if they can. I think for the most part most places are *mixed*. I think most schools are patchy: they think mental health important but they're not doing enough to really put systems and structures – and basically attitudes – in place. I do think there is a very small minority of schools whose behaviour is immoral. I would say two things. One is that everyone has an obligation to treat other people kindly – and you've got to do it first. No adult in a school should be complaining unless they have done the work of being kind to others *first*. Secondly, to balance this, they have got to expect that level of respect back. It's the quid pro quo. Sometimes people want the solutions to be elsewhere and they haven't actually looked at their *own* behaviour.

So, in short, we should plan and think through our conversations when feeding back. Before anything else, this section is about looking at – and indeed *planning* – our own behaviour. When I was an NQT, I was observed by a more experienced colleague who was an Advanced Skills Teacher (basically, when extra money was paid to amazing teachers so they'd stay in the classroom for longer periods). I thought the lesson was great – really great. I was probably what you might call 'unconsciously incompetent' at that stage. But by the time I'd received my feedback, I had torn my own lesson to shreds. However, I *still* felt a million dollars. The observer didn't *tell* me anything; she saw my enthusiasm and passion, she guided me to ask the right questions and I left with some really specific things to implement. What good would it have done to tell me all the deficits in my lesson? I'd just be left with gaps to fill and deficiencies to address. There is a place for being more direct, but it is about judging the repercussions for the person, their teaching and inevitably their students.

But, for this book, the more interesting thing is the role of compassion in this exchange. Being empathic and understanding the impact of overwhelmingly negative feedback would not only have done damage to my own self-confidence, but it would have impacted my teaching from that point onwards. It felt as if the observer was saying, 'Your efforts were great here. What do you think of this...?' By valuing my opinion and seeing me as someone who was just trying their best, she was *still* able to get me to the same endpoint. I suppose you could say my drive was through the roof: I had all the answers, but she came along with the right amount of soothe to help me focus and direct my ideas. Not a threat in sight.

Judgements and preference

Paul Gilbert makes a distinction between judgement and preference. Simply put:

> 'Being non-judgemental means not condemning, criticising, shaming or rejecting.'[32]

For me, judgements are often fused with emotions and feelings, whereas preferences are less bound, less intrinsic and more easily reconciled with personal values. I *love* this distinction, mainly because it destroys the integrity of basic 'judgements' on teachers and lessons. As soon as you set a judgement against your own preferences, you're in dangerous territory. Think about it this way: when we see something in a lesson, are

32. Gilbert, P. (2009) 'Introducing compassion-focused therapy', *Advances in Psychiatric Treatment* 15 (3) pp. 199–208.

we making a *judgement* from our own feelings and emotions, or are we noticing it in terms of our own personal *preference*? And when we 'judge' lessons (explicitly or implicitly), against what values and scales are we measuring? It's OK to have preferences – and discuss them openly in light of values – but I'm not sure if the same can be said as easily of making judgements (e.g. this person didn't do ___, therefore they must be ___'). We are so often told to separate the behaviour from the child, and not to bind it up in something intrinsic about the person, but we do precisely the opposite on those checklisted learning walks and observations.

Here, for me, is the key: ticks, crosses, reds, ambers, greens, positives and negatives are codified and correlated in Excel spreadsheets up and down the country as indicators of judgement on *teachers*. But they ought to be self-reflective (judgemental?) indicators for leadership teams and the effectiveness with which a vision has been conceived and communicated. From top to bottom, we need to have *preferences* for what we want to see in lessons – rooted firmly in our *values*. Alright, we might see things in lessons which might not match our personal *preferences*; but if they are in line with our values, who cares? This still leaves plenty of room for intrinsically valuable things for any school – things like clear structures and transparency. Tom Sherrington's *Learning Rainforest* addresses this magnificently; he makes a clear distinction between rainforests and plantations. Specifically, he says:

> 'My inclination is to suggest that a managed rainforest is the most appropriate metaphor for the system we should seek and the mindset we need to adopt for great teaching. It's the most aspirational; where idealism is not lost – it is just made real; where lush diversity is still the goal, provided core standards are met. In the managed rainforest, teachers and leaders are the rangers, walking the forest floor, making sure that anyone floundering is nurtured without imposing restrictions on others.' [33]

Just for a moment, reflect on the kind of school you work in. Is it like the one Sherrington describes? Or are things done and achieved through avoidance of guilt and shame? This need not be a conscious effort on the part of leaders – remember: *it's not their fault, but it is their responsibility!*

---

33. Sherrington, T. (2017) *The learning rainforest*. Woodbridge: John Catt Educational Ltd.

Planning compassionate conversations

More specifically, I think it's really worth using the three bubbles to think about how to give effective feedback. I've not really gone into this much, but I would say that the CFT model's most transformative effect on me was that it helped me to understand where others were coming from. I would even go to the extent of – prior to feeding back – thinking about the following:

Drive
What passion did you see in the lesson?
How did they demonstrate this?
How can you get them thinking about replicating or improving the things they love?
How can you make them co-authors of their own feedback?
What deliberate practice can you celebrate?
What questions can you ask to elicit the most reflective response?

Soothe
What sorts of things can you say or do to diffuse any 'high-stakes' narrative?
What elements of school life/the lesson/experience of the colleague can you recognise and explore?
Is the feedback happening in a 'summoning' system? Are colleagues having to 'come to the headteacher's office'?

Threat
How can we turn the threat into failing our core purpose (i.e. students not learning)?
How can we turn the threat from the teacher to the situation and the context (and, in effect, depersonalise it while still making it particular to the lesson)?

We can all think of any number of times when we have either gotten it wrong when giving feedback, or been on the receiving end of rubbish feedback. Once, during a 'mocksted' (when teams are brought in to 'inspect' a school in the same way an Ofsted team would), a colleague at my school – who I sought out for feedback – said 'Well, it wasn't "inadequate", and we saw lots of "inadequate" teaching during the day.' I don't know which is worse: the fact I was *happy* that my lesson wasn't 'inadequate' (phew), the fact that I felt the need to be externally validated about my intrinsic worth as a teacher, or the fact that the feedback started and ended there. I genuinely can't choose.

I do mean this: feedback should never *feel* negative. It might feel tough, but it should never feel *negative*. And there is a psychological foundation to this: we don't *need* an excuse to feel anxious most of the time; we're wired for it, and the primal threat part of our brain is not only the most basic but also the most powerful (remember the fire alarm analogy). Likewise, there is a psychological basis for positively framed feedback: life on the soothe-drive axis is infinitely preferable and productive, as it allows us to feel safe from threats and negatives when we are reflecting on making ourselves more effective (another thing which can so often be inherently threatening: 'I need to be improved!'). We all have things to improve on all of the time, and that should be celebrated, not set against a backdrop of 'If I fail then X will happen and it will say something intrinsic about me as a person or a professional.' And I do think part of this is about wider trust in schools as well: is there a risk that the observer will scuttle back to leadership and say how appalling it was?

Here, it's worth considering the *needs* of who you are observing. We all need to improve for our own sense of purpose, and for the students. But what we need emotionally in order to stir the fire in the belly is different. As a faculty head, I might even plot my team out in a table like this (I've added some backstory for context):

	Who are they?	Threats	Drive & Soothe	What did I see in the lesson?
Chris	52; teaching for 25 years; secure in practice; hasn't tended to engage in observational practice according to colleagues	Being instructed to do something for the sake of it Loss of agency and control	Loves literature and facilitating the students' thinking about his subject	• Some wonderful discussion • Were all of the students tuned in? • Was there an opportunity to develop ideas in writing?
Danny	30; teaching for 3 years; according to colleagues, scraped through his NQT year and continues to struggle; nice person but has low expectations	Being 'confirmed' as a useless behaviour manager Being told (again) his lesson lacks pace and purpose	Loves using technology as a way of engaging students; lights up when they smile	• Really nice use of the whiteboard with an interactive website – must steal (tell him I'm stealing...) • Started well but students lost focus – was this a pace thing? A lack of support? Reflect myself and then ask him
Helena	32; lead practitioner; highly competent according to colleagues; confident and students speak highly of her	Being told she's wrong Feeling like her 'status' as a top teacher is threatened	Loves reading about teaching and evidence-based learning	• Discussion and explanations really clear – although I'm unsure what X meant – ask her! • Culture feels great – noticing that even the less focused ones are being carried along too

	Who are they?	Threats	Drive & Soothe	What did I see in the lesson?
Lucy	23; trainee teacher; struggling with most of her classes in terms of behaviour; mentor has mentioned that she's been tearful in recent weeks	Being asked to think about whether teaching really is for her or whether she's 'right' for the school	Loves it when the students 'get it' – has a real passion for organising her teaching on paper: files, notes, seating plans	• Entry routine not in place and lesson needs more structure at the start • Some wonderful questions and discussions – students involved with this nicely in general

Of course, this is a fairly broad-stroke approach to something which is infinitely more complex. I've combined drive and soothe together here, but it's important to remember that soothing on its own might be making a hot drink, sitting in their room and going to them when feeding back, or asking questions about something maybe even unrelated to work – in other words, sharing your common humanity. For me, the most important is to think about how the 'threats' can be addressed in a way that is honest and constructive, and non-intrinsic. There's been a wave of training for middle and senior leaders around 'having difficult conversations' which I find unhelpful as it is oppositional – to the point that some seem to thrive on being able to have them, and stop at nothing to demonstrate their ability to do so.

There's also the distinction between coaching and mentoring as well. This is a useful distinction as it helps to think about what the needs of the other person are. A coach is more goal-oriented and specific in feedback, whereas a mentor is basically like Yoda, asking the mentee to reflect and guide their own improvement. My observer knew I was driven enough that I'd be in a position – with prodding – to find my own answers; whereas it might be that Lucy (above) needs a coach to be specific with strategies to help her manage her class at the start. I'd start by having a title, date and a 'do now' task on the board *every* lesson to get the students into a place where they can securely come in and engage in the learning. I think Lucy might get a certain sense of soothe and safety from specific strategies to help her establish her classroom routines (before asking her about other great parts of the lesson); whereas what might soothe the others and help them to drive their own development is more question-led and open-ended. I have to say, though, that I might give Danny some specific things to put in place as 'quick wins' to unlock the potential in the class.

It's key to remember that feedback can never be entirely unilateral if we are to meet someone's human needs; to some degree it needs to come from the other person. You can't possibly know the intent behind every aspect of what you've seen, nor can you really make any entirely accurate assessments about the immediate outcome (don't get me started on that ridiculous notion of 'rapid and sustained' progress). Co-construction isn't about stepping over unhelpful aspects of a lesson; it's about involving the other person in a way that empowers. At the end of the day, you're not in that room with the students as much as they are, and they are *more important* to the progress of that class than you are!

C. Connections
with students

'Compassion is not a relationship between the healer and the wounded.
It's a relationship between equals. Only when we know our own darkness
well can we be present with the darkness of others. Compassion becomes
real when we recognize our shared humanity.'

Pema Chödrön

Professor Joe Elliott – an expert in special education needs and
behaviour at *Durham University* – said something really interesting to
me about cultural norms. He observed that in other cultures such as in
China or South America, behaviour isn't an issue; but in fundamentally
liberal societies such as the UK or USA, the rights of the individual are
so intertwined with how we see the world that it has led to some of the
things we are confronted with as teachers in the classroom. What follows
is *not* my way of saying how we can be nice to students; it is my attempt
to articulate how to enhance the chances of a positive and meaningful
classroom culture.

I remember writing an essay about motivation during my PGCE – what
a bloody nightmare. Dear me, there's all kinds of rabbit holes you can
find yourself down on that particular issue. For present purposes, I just
want to point out one thing which might sound obvious, but I'll say it

anyway: what motivates us as teachers and what motivates students are not necessarily the same. The issue of placing outcomes at the epicentre of education is that leaders and teachers are at risk of allowing learning to be defined by them, and unfortunately – for whatever reason – not all students are intrinsically motivated by a grade (some are actually turned off by them). Anyhow, as a trainee, I signed up for every teaching union going: they were all free. One even gave me a book: the brilliant Sue Cowley's *Getting the Buggers to Behave*. I read the opening few pages – and was filled with such confidence that I put it down and didn't revisit it until the summer after I finished my training. As I recall, those pages alluded to standing in front of a class with certainty and presumption that things will go the way you want them to and that you'll carry the class with you.

A magic formula? No. But it tapped into something I already knew: I had to carry positivity and realism into the classroom with me and be authentic. I didn't know why; I just wanted to do it that way. I do think there is one key rule, though: *always give students something to lose – make them feel as if they're valued and that you've invested something in them*. It can be a simple question, an acknowledgement of a common interest, a nod, a 'You OK? Sure?' at the right moment. It's soothing, and is the shortcut to drive.

Again, now would be a very useful place to bring in my discussion with Dr Chris Irons about the potential for using the CFT Approach in the classroom.

How do you see this working in an educational setting?

Chris: In many different ways. From my perspective, this is a powerful approach because it can be applied across many levels of the school system. For example, this could help teachers to be the best version of themselves in the classroom, but also help them to navigate the common stresses and strains of their jobs. But it's also how this approach has the potential to be used in other areas. This could include how to help children to understand and work with their own minds – something that we don't do very well at the moment, in my opinion. But it could also be used in thinking about how colleagues support each other, how staff in leadership roles think about and help more junior staff, even through to the philosophy of the school around attainment and developing well-rounded, kind young people.

What about applying the model for teachers specifically?

Chris: If you ask teachers why they wanted to get in to the profession, it's most often because they had a great passion to want to be helpful, to support kids to be the best version of themselves. So in many ways it is a compassionate motivation towards others that is central to why teachers want to do what they do. The problem is that this motivation then gets caught up in an education system that can, at times, be toxic – the stress of class sizes and targets, financial cutbacks at schools, managing of emotional and educational difficulties of a diverse group of pupils. Unfortunately – through no fault of anyone – this can then lead to burnout and a diminishing of this initial compassionate motivation. We can lose access to a healthy functioning of our drive system, and get caught in a threat system that can cause teachers a lot of distress.

So at a fundamental level, compassionate motivation – and an understanding of the things that might get in the way of this – sit centrally in how we can use this model to support teachers, and reflect on the schooling system more broadly. On a more specific level to teachers, the CFT approach can then help teachers to consider how they want to be – what their intention is, how they can focus on being the best version of themselves as a teacher (and for that matter, as a colleague). The approach can help reflection on what stops us from being that version of ourselves, and the practices of compassionate mind training (CMT) help us to balance our threat system in a way that then allows us to access our compassionate self, and start using this on a day-to-day basis.

I also think the model can provide a useful framework for teachers to think about and work with their students. For example, once teachers become aware of the three-system model, it can then be used as a way to think about why certain children may be struggling in class. For many children this will be to do with their threat systems being too powerful. We know that whilst some kids will struggle to learn and participate in class because they become inhibited by anxiety, low self-confidence, other children will struggle because they they're afraid of failure and are full of shame. But it's not just the threat system that is important – some children will struggle to learn if they're not experiencing enough drive system. This could be because they don't experience emotions of the drive system (e.g. excitement) about the subject being taught, or the way it's being taught doesn't tap in to a sense of challenge, achievement or desire for attainment. This then brings a sense of why trying to help children feel a sense of safeness (soothing system) is so important. This is something that teachers can help to create on behalf of the child in the classroom itself. Or we can start teaching children to do it through their own experiential practice (e.g. of mindfulness, soothing breathing, imagery and so on).

Coming back to the class teacher though: to do some of the above – to hold in mind the different needs of children in a large class – is tricky in itself. So this is where many of the practices of CFT can help to support teachers remaining grounded, self-supportive and calm (as much as is possible in a classroom) so that they have access to their new brain abilities to think, reflect and empathise. It is these qualities that then help teachers to hold the children in their class in a flexible, wise way, without feeling overwhelmed. An important aspect linked to this is how teachers can manage the emotional play-out between you and the child. And the tricky thing of course is that it's easy when you like the student – things flow quite nicely there. It's when you work with a student who pushes your buttons, and each of us will have different buttons that will be pressed. For some teachers, it will be the angry kids or the lippy kid who they struggle to work with, whereas other teachers are fine with that – they can have that all day long and they've got that confidence to switch it around. Some teachers will find the introverted child the most threat triggering for them. So it's about helping teachers to begin to recognise their own patterns and things that trigger them in terms of the classroom and teaching itself. But also outside of the classroom: what are the things that will trigger our threat systems? Then we're back to motivation, really, and that real sense that compassion connects you with.

This was my point of departure when considering teacher-student connections in particular: what follows is my rationalisation of effective teacher-student relationships within the CFT model. I think it makes sense; I hope you will too. I'll begin by thinking at the school level, and then working my way down to classroom management, and even one-to-one relationships.

Rules and regs, regs and rules

In the opening of his book *When the Adults Change, Everything Changes*, Paul Dix[34] makes a really important point about the thing that unites all great schools: they have a uniformity of approach to behaviour and culture. I'm sure you'll agree: clear behaviour systems create the space for more meaningful things to happen. What I love about his book is that his suggestions and strategies all speak to minimising threat and maximising the space for soothing to happen before learning can happen. I agree 100% with Dix: rules aren't 'patronising or limiting' but they create a base for more meaningful things to happen. There's no point in labouring this here; I don't really think it's a debate.

Mary Welford[35] makes this point brilliantly: behaviour systems aren't there to punish; they are there to create a predictable and consistent environment. Such systems allow conversations between staff and students to take place that needn't take on a threatening frame. However, I do think that this can be pushed too far. I've seen schools that are almost entirely proudly *defined* by their behaviour systems, and there is absolutely no question that they establish what look like effective learning environments – and they allow colleagues who are less proficient in behaviour management to do the same. I don't dispute that in some contexts, for some of the life stages of a school, such measures are a step in the right direction. I'd argue, though, that an over-reliance on a behaviour system means that it can begin to define everyone's entire experience of school. By this, I mean that behaviours can be adjusted to avoid punishment but without necessarily encouraging

34. Dix, P. (2017) *When the adults change, everything changes*. Carmarthen: Crown House Publishing Ltd.
35. Welford, M. and Langmead, K. (2015) 'Compassion-based initiatives in educational settings', *Educational and Child Psychology* 32 (1) pp. 71–80.

the pursuit of learning. Peps Mccrea[36] makes a pretty alarming point about learning that is worth thinking about here too: if something isn't contributing to the learning, it's taking something away. A similar pattern begins to emerge, doesn't it? Something which started out as an attempt to promote learning can run the risk of *defining* learning, with not-so-great consequences.

Obviously, no behaviour system is a guarantee of success. All a system can do is provide a framework for consistency and the right environment. Nor do specific things intrinsically lead to success, such as rewards boards, attendance charts, merit systems etc. – they only work if they are a framework for adults to genuinely tap into the drive-soothe systems of their students. As a colleague of mine always says: 'People don't follow systems; people follow people.' What does this mean, then? Well, again, there isn't a great deal you can do about your school's behaviour policy; but you can begin to understand the context and use it to your advantage.

My Fortress of Solitude

There's something narcissistic about teaching, I think. You stand up, and you are the expert in the room for about 3–4 hours a day. I think that's cool. But my favourite thing about teaching is that you can truly be the author of your own script – 'you establish what you establish', to quote Bill Rogers[37] – and you can create the conditions for your own show as well (at least to an extent). Here, I'll explore some of the things that I've found to be effective in my classroom, with some kind of psychological explanation.

At every level, whatever you term 'behaviour management', for me it needs to exist on the drive-soothe axis if it is to be sustainable and meaningful. Too much threat ('If you don't do X then I will do Y' or 'Right, you'll end up in X if you don't stop Y') taps into negative and threatening narratives, and although it might yield some short-term results, and

36. Mccrea, P. (2017) *Memorable teaching: leveraging memory to build deep and durable learning in the classroom.* Scotts Valley, CA: CreateSpace Independent Publishing Platform.
37. Sherrington, T. (2015) 'Behaviour management: a Bill Rogers top 10', *Teacherhead* [blog]. Available at: www.bit.ly/2DulcrQ (Accessed 12 Oct 2018).

even breed long-term compliance, it won't facilitate learning. This, I think, taps into something in Daniel Willingham's *Why Don't Students Like School?* when he notes that the brain is designed for avoidance of thought, although that isn't the end of the story. Willingham points out:

'We will seek out opportunities to think, but we are selective in doing so; we choose problems that pose some challenge but that seem likely to be solvable, because these are the problems that lead to feelings of pleasure and satisfaction.'[38]

Why is this relevant here? Because I think the choices that Willingham talks about are – explicitly or implicitly – coloured to some extent by the students' perceptions of their environment, such as:

- Does this teacher want to be here?
- Am I likely to be doing something worthwhile this lesson?
- Does this teacher know who I am – or care?
- Is there a culture in this classroom that I want to buy into?

A purposeful culture gives us our best shot of giving our students a safe platform from which to engage with the learning. Here are some things which I think link most closely to this:

Relentless positivity: Just like behaviour systems, our classroom cultures should be designed to capture and channel as much positivity as possible. As a rule of thumb I believe that positive reinforcement should dominate negativity in terms of quantity. Before exploring positivity, I'd place two conditions on the use of what I had previously wrongly called 'negative reinforcement' when I was referring to giving someone a telling off. Negative reinforcement – strictly speaking – is the removal of something positive when an undesirable behaviour is displayed so we can 'remedy' it. This got me thinking about what I was trying to refer to. In truth, it's basically a reference to negativity or recognition of something undesirable (e.g. missing homework or poor behaviour) with a view to disciplining someone; technically, it's called 'positive punishment.' Anyway, two conditions on 'positive punishment':

---

38. Willingham, D. T. (2010) *Why don't students like school?* San Francisco, CA: Jossey-Bass.

1. **On a class level, it should be used sparingly and candidly** – for example, when you're halfway through a lesson and it doesn't feel right – too many are not on their game. 'Right, 3-2-1. Ladies and gents, this isn't us today; our efforts aren't where they should be yet. I need X, Y and Z – let's get this done and get back to being our best selves please.' **Why?** Psychologically, a mass-bollocking runs the risk of defusing responsibility and students thinking 'That's not me'. The situation above describes the teacher addressing the classroom culture as a single entity – something positive we can all be part of. Students aren't daft; they might feel completely undervalued individually or just collectively feel like the lesson is a failure.

2. **On an individual level, it should be within clear boundaries, and with clear reference to the student's choice rather than the individual – however irritated we feel.** 'Our expectation was that _____, and you haven't met it. Why?' **Why?** Because making it about a behaviour – as you have probably been told – separates it from something intrinsic about them. When it's something intrinsic, I think that taps into threat-based responses much more easily because it feels less changeable and more permanent. This is immensely counterintuitive and frustrating, probably!

Recently, a trainee said something to me which didn't sound right, but I couldn't really disagree. She said, 'I've been told that for that hour you're with a class, you've got to make it seem like there's *nowhere else in the world* you'd rather be – like you are *absolutely thrilled* to be with them.' I wrestled with it in my mind until I understood. Just like a behaviour system isn't a guarantee of success, but a chance-booster, so is relentless positivity. What it will do is garner as much buy-in to capture the group as possible. A one-to-one compassionate understanding is not possible when you're stood in front of 30 people. But what you can do is appeal to the drive and soothe of the class as a single entity.

One thing you can do, then, is shape the atmosphere in your own classroom with your tone and body language. I would thoroughly recommend Doug Lemov's *Teach Like a Champion*[39] because it offers a

---

39. Lemov, D. (2010) *Teach like a champion.* San Francisco, CA: Jossey-Bass.

range of very tangible things you can be doing which appeal to the drive and soothe of a class. Things like having books out, having a 'do now' task on the board with a clear, routinised focus, and a clear (stretched out) ten-second countdown for the title to be written down and the do now to be underway all imply focus, calm, control and purpose. All these things appeal to soothe and drive: 'I know what's going to happen in this lesson, and I know I'm likely to do something worthwhile.'

Just like schools throw up any number of infuriating and upsetting things, so does being in a room with 30 students. We can't avoid it, but we can try to notice and hear ourselves when we speak. So when homework isn't complete, or Bradley still hasn't written his title, or someone has come in late, it makes no sense to allow a lesson to be dominated or – worse still – *defined* by a minority of negativity. Yes, it is hugely irritating when the vast majority haven't done their homework or whatever you've asked of them. But that is the fact; if we're that bothered, we can chase up/contact parents/hold back at break or lunch later on – but that is not the business of now. Even if someone is incessantly talking, then again, it's about making expectations clear with that purposeful tone, saying, 'Chris, come on – let's get going.' Depersonalising this – maybe not even making eye contact in the first instance – is a way of being clear without necessarily making it threatening and personal (more on this later).

We've *all* done it – we've *all* probably fallen into negative dialogues with our students out of irritation and/or a lack of their motivation and drive. But we need to recognise how we feel, and step away. A long time ago, I remember getting about ten minutes into a lesson, and I just felt utterly irritated. So did the kids. It wasn't until I caught myself after and had a think:

- Students were late from assembly.
- There was no clearly defined starting point (date/title not on board).
- About 8/30 had done their homework; I launched into a diatribe about lack of motivation.
- Noisy students were noisy during my opening explanation.
- I spent five minutes ranting about a lack of attendance at my after-school revision session.

I'd not stood back and reflected – I didn't have the insight. In her professional capacity, I stunned my wife Philippa by saying 'Give me an estimate – what proportion of positive reinforcement and positive punishment should I try to have in my classroom?' I had to push her quite hard to get an answer, but she said 'about 90%'. When you put this in the context of our threat-addled brain, as well as the unknowable complexities of the lives of everyone in our classroom, it makes absolute sense to be as positive as we can to move the lesson in a direction that is purposeful.

Passive steering: This is another one of those things that really effective behaviour managers probably do without noticing it. It's not about avoiding confrontation, but about knowing when confrontation is effective. As my mate would say, 'Think about the hill you want to die on!' In short, if a student is talking when they shouldn't be, it's about directing your explanation to that part of the room, standing nearby, a quiet tap on the desk to passively let them know you're watching, or even staring about a metre *above* the table that is talking and saying, 'ladies/ gentlemen' rather than singling anyone out as a way of perpetuating that positivity. In his work, Graham Nuthall[40] recognised that students:

> 'live in a personal and social world of their own in the classroom. They whisper to each other and pass notes. They spread rumours about girlfriends and boyfriends, they organize their after-school social life, continue arguments that started in the playground. They care more about how their peers evaluate their behaviour than they care about the teacher's judgement.'

This, for me, is why students often hate being challenged by a teacher: losing face in front of their mates. Directly challenging all of the time is face-threatening. Passive acknowledgement that things aren't as you expect is a way of being in command, but not at anyone's expense, so to speak.

Planning for productive classroom cultures

You can also start to conceptualise your classroom culture with the CFT model. Just as the most effective schools have a clarity over their ethos and values which are being lived out, I think you can begin to unpick the culture in your own classes too. As a collective, the narratives that a

---

40. www.bit.ly/2SFX675

group of students can buy into can be extremely unhelpful: I would say that when I've struggled with a class, I've always found unpicking and reshaping cultures through the *combinations* of students much more difficult than on an individual level. For sake of example, as a collective, let's imagine you've inherited an incredibly difficult year 9 class that have been passed from pillar to post over the last 6 months. They've become disenchanted with your subject, and lessons invariably end with an incredible amount of sanctions and negative consequences. You could start to think about turning things around like so:

Planning for classroom culture – initial questions

Drive

How do they feel about the subject? Why? What is that based on?
If I were walking past as a neutral observer, what would I see and why?
How can I start to give them positive and meaningful experiences?
What kind of learner behaviours do they display? What is this telling me?
How can I show them that they can succeed?

Soothe

How can I establish a climate of (psychological and physical) safety and fairness?
If appropriate, how can I acknowledge that the subject has been tough, but explain that I will try to make things different (and am confident about doing so)?
How can I embed a sense of joy into my lessons?
What balance of structure and freedom is right for these students?

Threat

What are the class's fears about the subject?
What narratives persist about them?
What do they say about themselves?
Are there any individuals who are particularly unhelpful in terms of the class's culture? How can I address that quietly and without threat?
How can I expect negative behaviours to manifest?
How can I intercept negativity through seating plans and structures?

Strategising classroom culture for a tough class

Drive

Praise effort
Notice progress from one point to another and highlight it.
Model and work through examples as a class – be deliberate and precise in how to succeed.
Leave room for choices where possible when completing a task- levels of support/task type.

Soothe

Reassurance, consistency and routines will be key to establishing trust.
Build relationships – share a joke/use personal anecdotes.
Greet at the door where possible.
Use music for extended periods of silent work.

Threat

Identify narratives of students or as a class – turn them on their heads: 'Oh, I've never heard that about your class'.
Where appropriate, speak to individuals quietly and privately – unpick individual narratives and build relationships.
Build up to tasks deliberately and be precise about expectations – minimise risk of failure, especially to begin with.
Celebrate any kind of meaningful success.

This isn't about manipulation: it's about recognising the realities of the situations that we face. I do genuinely think that classes function as organisms in their own right. Those questions that perhaps more experienced teachers ask (such as the following) have real foundations; they respect that culture is a 'thing' to be recognised, addressed and cultivated:

- Who are my main 'influencers'?
- Which combinations work? Which don't?
- When are the class 'tougher'? How might I need to adapt my lessons?
- Who is interested in what? How can I add flavour and spice with a little bit of a personal touch?

So, how can you be compassionate to 30 people at once? By acknowledging that as a *collective*, they are one single entity. I think that once you begin to respect the culture of a class in its own right, you have a much better chance of being able to understand the individuals involved more meaningfully.

From me to you: individual student-teacher relationships

'Compassion is the keen awareness of the interdependence of all things.'
Thomas Merton

What I'm referring to in this section is the one-to-one conversations you have with students during, before or after a lesson. Where possible, I think talking to small groups of students about their behaviour in a lesson just perpetuates the problem of shared responsibility: 'Don't worry, we're in this together. He's just having a pop at all of us so we're going to smirk and giggle to save face in front of each other.'

I'd argue that establishing the right culture at classroom level is interwoven with those one-to-one relationships you have with your students. Again, much of this section is part theory and part based on my own experiences; taking the two together leaves us with more than the sum of its parts, I hope. To save you going backwards, here is the definition of compassion for our present purposes:

'a sensitivity to suffering in self and others, with a commitment to try to alleviate and prevent it.'

To acknowledge that all behaviour is communication is not the same thing as to excuse it. Compassion is *hard*: being compassionate to students is really, really bloody hard, especially when you have depleted energy levels yourself. I've already mentioned above the idea that we ought to start with ourselves and our own contexts. First and foremost, compassion is *inward* looking; the truth is that we will naturally bond and relate to some students more than others for all kinds of reasons. I'm not sure we can deny that. As hokey as it sounds, what we do have in common is our *humanity*, so it's perhaps slightly ironic that to get to that place, we need to acknowledge our own feelings of distance and – to a certain extent – discomfort. What I mean is basically saying to yourself, 'Yes, Daniel is incredibly frustrating and I feel like he's sabotaged my lessons time and time again. It's difficult for me to be compassionate here.'

To walk a mile (even a yard, actually) in everybody else's shoes is impossible in the context of a classroom. I don't think it's a mantra for teachers to live out all day every day, either. What I would say, however, is that to notice difficulties and to acknowledge our role in being able to alleviate a student's suffering is enough; they'll recognise you doing it. Here, it's important to recognise that some find it more difficult than others to be on the receiving end of compassionate behaviour; in short, they associate friendliness and safety with letting a guard down.[41]

Think of it like this: based on a person's life experiences, it is entirely possible to link feeling 'relaxed' with feeling 'threatened'; when one relaxes, they are perhaps slightly more vulnerable to shock or being taken advantage of. Imagine the depth and scale of impact in some of the circumstances our young people face in their homes every day. Research has even shown the influence of trauma and neglect on young minds.[42] The environment doesn't need to be defined by threat in order to achieve its goals; in the short term – and in some cases – it's best to retreat and give students space. I've been with students when they are clearly upset by something, and me trying to be soothing and caring would just have

---

41. Gilbert, P. (2014) 'The origins and nature of compassion focused therapy', *British Journal of Clinical Psychology* 53 (1) pp. 6–41.
42. Children Welfare Information Gateway (2015) *Understanding the effects of maltreatment on brain development.* Washington, DC: US Department of Health and Human Services. Available at: www.bit.ly/2BuHmde (Accessed 12 Oct 2018).

led to an explosion. In other words, there's a time and a place for these conversations to take place.

A note on 'restorative justice' conversations

When I speak to other teachers, there's often a harboured resentment of 'restorative justice' and the like: 'Justice? This kid has just ruined my lesson, been horrifically rude to me and undermined the learning of the others in the room, whose progress – which I am being held over a barrel for, incidentally – will suffer.' Sound familiar? This is another one of those terms which probably started out as a good idea (although the name is less than desirable) but now in some contexts (consciously or unconsciously) is used as a by-product of placing sole responsibility back on the teacher. Frankly, students and teachers have a peculiar kind of asymmetrical relationship: we have a job to do together, but we're doing more than just imparting knowledge. So, as well as having our own self-awareness, I'd ask what has been communicated to teachers around these restorative conversations to put them at ease. Imagine having a conversation in the presence of a third party who has little or no understanding of what has transpired, when you had likely exercised your professional judgement to the best of your ability (not to mention that the student probably feels outnumbered and on trial anyway). I'm not saying that a meaningfully positive outcome is impossible. I'm just saying that the odds are stacked against the chances of it happening. Yes, teachers are the adults. Yes, teachers are crucial in driving these relationships. But I'd argue that there can be a complete lack of support around these conversations, not to mention students' understanding of their *own* emotional needs.

In any case, I'd still go in through soothe: 'Look, it went wrong today. From my perspective, I thought _____. How about you, what went wrong for you?' When that is established, you can direct the conversation where it needs to go.

When you hit the brick wall with students

In her professional capacity, my wife Philippa is incredibly empathetic when she speaks about people. She often flips narratives on their head using compassion; in fact, given people's life experiences, it is often *hardly surprising* that they are where they are. That, ladies and gents, is the most inconvenient of truths, but it is one we have to face. In this sense, the first time my own therapy really helped me with a student was when I just felt like I had hit a wall with them. When I say 'hit a wall' I mean I felt utterly exasperated and at the end of my tether with what I would actually be able to do.

Matthew was in Year 11, and I'd taught him for about half a term previously when he was in Year 9. He was a 'below the radar' type then: he had flashes of real flair and insight into what we were studying but was often too busy distracting himself and others away to engage on a consistent basis. I began to notice during mock exams during Year 10 that his apathy was turning into full-blown rejection of learning; he'd sit there for hours not writing anything. During lessons in Year 11, he'd often opt out of what we were doing in any way possible. Time after time, I'd hit a wall. He *genuinely* seemed not to care about his learning or consequences in the short, medium or long term. I unthinkingly kept him back for break, with nothing to go on but my own irritation. He rightly assumed he was in for a bollocking, and a trip into the future where failure would lead to the abyss.

I knew I needed to distance myself from my anger, and I tried to do the most compassionate thing I could: I used the circles. I thought to myself that I had nothing to lose, so I explained the model to him before asking him some questions to begin to get him to think about it for himself. I've summarised each on the next page.

Threat, drive, soothe: a worked example

Drive

Didn't care about education; didn't feel like he would achieve even if he tried.
Had no ambitions or desires; he didn't feel they were achievable anyway.
Perceived that parents had no real interest in how he was doing – a real lack of motivation from home.

Soothe

No real way of feeling safe in a classroom space – felt exposed.
No/few relationships with teachers that felt productive, long term and safe.

Threat

Didn't want to do 'nothing' with his life.
Didn't know how he could avoid doing 'nothing' with his life.
Hated getting things wrong – fears about not being good enough had been confirmed to him previously in his results.

Beginning to see Matthew in these terms really helped me to unpick what was going on, as well as fire *my own* drive system when it came to helping him. I felt myself wanting to slip into the old narrative: 'Well, if you keep doing this, you will *definitely* fail' – which surely would have just fired his threat system and shut him down even more. We've all heard the term 'learned helplessness', and that is what Matthew was presenting me with; but it was buried underneath some really difficult narratives to unpick.

He didn't really associate soothe with trustworthiness, either, so that was something I had to tread carefully with.

I had very little to show him in his book in terms of where he had succeeded, and very little in the way of positive contributions that he had made to demonstrate to him that success was possible. I found the most useful place to start was putting him at ease: I made it clear that I'd kept him behind not for a telling off, but a conversation. I know this might not work for all of the students all of the time, but I'd say acknowledging reality and acknowledging humanity is the best way to start. It went something like this:

Soothe:	Drive:
Acknowledged the situation for what it was: annoyance of being kept behind	Asked about the future – what did a positive future look like?
Led by him: asked him how he felt right now – be honest!	Asked about the focus of where he wanted to go
Acknowledged that he was irritated by me, perhaps	Asked about things he wanted to achieve with support – asked about
Acknowledged previous positive efforts	things he wanted to steer clear of as well (careful to walk the threat line here)
Tried to make eye contact (but didn't push it)	
Slightly softer tone of voice	

No, this didn't magically transform Matthew overnight – of course it didn't. At times, there'll be students that associate soothe with adverse feelings owing to other things in their lives, so we need to know when to get close – so to speak – and when to move away. The point isn't to predict or even know every student's emotional starting point; the point is to be sensitive that it might not always be clear. In truth, it helped me just as much as it helped him, and it gave me a way in. The authenticity of the relationship that follows is where the real work is done. At times, too, I think just having a conversation with soothe at its heart is enough. I could probably have just stopped after the soothe at that moment; that was what helped me make that initial breakthrough. Mary Myatt's words are ringing in my ears as I type: *treat people as people first*. Only then can any sort of meaningful business take place. I suppose the point of all of this is that there are any number of barriers – some self-imposed, some completely out of anyone's control – that stop a student from giving their best. We need to do our best to make ourselves aware of how some of these barriers might manifest. If nothing else, this, for me, is the very essence of teaching.

It's clear that Matthew's wider life and attitudes were a huge influence on his approach to school. At some level, we need to build a better understanding to be able to unpick some of these things. At this point, it would be really useful to bring in the thoughts of Natalie Jewitt, a clinical psychologist working with young people, families and schools to build awareness and knowledge around mental health. Dr Jewitt runs Jenby's, an independent psychology service for children and parents. She has also established a platform to begin working with schools to improve understanding of the issues we face.

What's your approach to working with young people?

Natalie: When I first meet with a family who have concerns about their child, my primary focus is to build up an understanding of all the interacting layers around the child. It is important to keep in mind that children do not exist in isolation: they have many interactions, experiences and relationships around them – with parents, siblings, friends, and teachers. It is essential that we explore these layers to build up an understanding of how they may relate to the presenting difficulties.

Connecting with teachers about individual pupils can be tricky at times; not because they don't want to, but because they have limited time to do so with the demands of their role as a teacher. This is one of the reasons I started to develop the Jenby's in Schools project, which is a whole-school approach to promoting and improving child mental health in schools. I wanted to develop a way of joining with schools and parents to equip and empower the next generation with the knowledge, understanding and tools to look after their mental health. I was aware that teachers really value mental health education and were keen to join with mental health professionals like myself to fill this crucial gap in education, but this needed to be done in a way that worked with the limited time they had.

How can teachers do more to support the mental health of young people in front of them?

Natalie: Teachers often already have a lot of knowledge about mental health and want to be able to help children to develop their understanding, but for some reason – maybe because in the past we've always said 'Oh, that's mental health; refer to the professionals' – they've not had the confidence to know that it is OK to talk about a young person's experience of anxiety or low mood. There's often lots of ways they can help before referring to mental health services. The criteria to get an NHS service has increased exponentially, often putting children in a place where they are left to feel worse before they can get any help, which is just madness. In my practice I see children a lot earlier; more lower-level anxiety, friendship issues or relationship problems. Another reason for developing the Jenby's in Schools project was that I felt there was a chunk of my work that didn't need to be done by a clinical psychologist in terms of the basic psycho-education stuff and equipping children with the tools to manage 'big feelings'. You don't need to be a clinical psychologist to be able to do that; with the right training and support, this can be done both within school and with parents or carers – and be hugely beneficial.

I have a slide in all my training session presentations where I ask teaching staff to give me a rough percentage of pupils in their school that have mental health – but as they turn to their neighbour to discuss and come up with a percentage, I flick to the next slide which has '100%' in massive text! That's one of the crucial things that we've really tried to challenge and break down: the assumption that we don't need to talk about mental health in children unless there's a problem. Actually, that's not true: we *all* have mental health, we all experience anxiety, we all experience 'big feelings'. So, if we don't equip children to understand that and be able to manage that, then in my opinion we're failing them. We need to rethink child mental health and focus more on prevention work we can do – prevention will always be better than cure.

How does your project work then?

Natalie: The project involves providing whole-school mental health training to help equip all staff with the knowledge and understanding of how to help their pupils look after their mental health. Each school involved has two Jenby's facilitators who are trained by myself to run Jenby's in Schools groups on both understanding emotions and anxiety – with six pupils in each group. I support all facilitators throughout the running of the project and provide regular supervision. It is primarily a preventative project for all children to access. I often talk about how we wouldn't wait till a child's teeth are all falling out before we explained the importance of brushing their teeth and limiting sugar, so we shouldn't be doing this with their mental health.

More than anything, we need to address confidence levels to talk about mental health. As professionals, we need to join together. Mental health should definitely be on the curriculum for all children. Those skills are so important in life, particularly in light of social change – and we know that a *lot* has changed. Social media has changed; the pressure that children are under has changed; even just the make-up of families has changed. All those changes have increased the strain on mental health, but we haven't done anything with that. We've not adjusted the curriculum or even equipped parents to deal with that, and I believe this can only be done by working together.

If I had to pick one thing that I'd want all children, parents and teachers to know more about it would be anxiety. We all feel anxiety from time to time. It's a normal, functional and even at times helpful emotion. It becomes problematic when it starts impacting on day-to-day life. One of the things the Jenby's in Schools project aims to do is to help children recognise when they feel anxiety, understand why changes happen in their bodies, and really importantly empower them with tools to manage this throughout their school years and beyond.

There are profound implications to what Dr Jewitt says, especially in light of social change. Mental health isn't necessarily alien in schools in terms of awareness, but it does make me question the extent of the understanding in our schools and classrooms. In other words, what might a useful discussion around mental health look like for a teacher speaking with their students? More broadly, I think, we need to prepare young people for the world they face not only economically, but *psychologically* too. Adrian Bethune – a pioneer in the area of mental health (particularly in the primary sector) – spoke with real clarity about his own experiences with depression and anxiety, and his words really struck a chord with my own experiences:

> I had never experienced anything like that before. I was a typically 'happy-go-lucky' kind of person, and quite optimistic. It really threw me. And basically I had two moments of clarity during this period. The first one was that I'd worked extremely hard at school: my GCSEs, my A levels, then university; I felt like I had all this knowledge from the various qualifications I gained, but none of that knowledge was helping me get out of my anxiety or depression. Secondly, when your mental health goes, it is the most important thing – your lens on the whole world. And when it's not right it impacts on *everything*: your relationships, your sleep, what you eat – everything.

Presently, we're often gearing our young people to think of education as only important for jobs and qualifications; whether this is implicit or explicit in the experience of young people in our schools and classrooms, I'd say it's not a healthy world-view to promote. We need to give young people opportunities to learn about what mental health *really* is, and how they can look after themselves.

Emotional literacy

The other night, my little boy was crying. He wouldn't stop. It was 3.37am when I looked at the clock, and my stomach lurched: 'Oh crap, I'm up in three hours to start work for the day, and my sleep is ruined.' I wanted to cry, and I was totally unable to soothe him. My body was tense, and it can't have been pleasant for him either. The next day, when I was chatting to Philippa about it, she told me that toddlers (and babies) need *us* to work their feelings out for them. It reminded me of when I was trying to tell a student off around a year ago. She looked like she was going to thump me. I was frustrated, and I was being too confrontational. All that happened was a slow aggression accumulated across her face. Perhaps all she'd known was aggression and threat, and the safest way of dealing with it was to come back at someone. I'd have been terrified to look at my teacher in an intimidating way at school; she wasn't. She needed me to soothe before being able to access any of her drive. To some extent, I think the same can be said for all young people: they need us to do some emotional articulating for them. There's a lot of work to be done around this particular issue (at least promoting a proper awareness of this in schools), but it's worth having a brief word on this. Although our own threat systems and fatigue can get in the way of us understanding, we have to remember that *all* behaviour is essentially communication.

At classroom level: For now, I think it's useful to think of yourself as a conductor: you can't deal with every single issue in front of you, so it's more about steering away from some avenues of tension and towards positivity as much as is possible. The 'relentless positivity' discussed above is about sometimes giving students a space to work things out for themselves. I always say to myself, 'acknowledge and move; come back later.' On a classroom level, I think it's about keeping pace and purpose as much as possible, and remembering to revisit things on an individual level when the opportunity arises.

Although they codify effective teaching, teacher instruction books often miss what underpins the strategies psychologically. The key, I think, is being calm, purposeful and energetic in the right amounts, at the right time. Whatever it is, consistency is the key. There'll be times when it feels chaotic (sometimes predictably if they come from PE – sorry, PE teachers), and it's less straightforward to create calm and clarity. This is where – despite your own emotions and possibly anxieties – your outside projection is crucial. Knowing when to acknowledge distractions, laugh along or play it down is a really tough call to make. Sometimes, a daft comment from a student can be laughed off and acknowledged to bring energy and purpose to a classroom; but obviously there needs to be a line with unhelpful things that students say.

In terms of the three bubbles model on a classroom level, it's really worthwhile to reflect on the behaviour of the group as an entity. There are definitely different kinds of energy that a class can exude. Sometimes, calm, silent reflection can be really useful; and sometimes, something 'busy' – such as a ranking exercise on a whiteboard or in exercise books – can be a useful way of focusing pent-up energy. In truth, it's difficult to write this, as teaching is so context dependent that it has to be down to individual teachers to develop their own inner barometer in terms of the levels of energy in a room. The key difference to this book, I think, is that with the CFT model, you can begin to think about where behaviours – including your own – come from, and how to respond to the emotions you or the students might be feeling.

If I were to codify my own recommendations to open lessons in a soothing and driven manner, for example, I'd say the following:

Always:	
1. Be at the door, greet, have books out and ready or at least have a designated student(s) to distribute books	
2. Have a 'do now' on the board, a greeting, a 'rule off' reminder, and the date and title	
Class needs to be calmed:	1. Can consult in quiet pairs (don't give them anything to 'bounce' against), answer recap questions – short sentences
	2. Have three key words on the board – ask to write down and explain which one is the odd one out
	3. Have a picture of an effective piece of work from the previous lesson on the board – write down three areas of strength and one area of development for the piece
	All these are clear, focused and have irrefutable expectations and outcomes. The more consistency we have, the less room for rebellion there is and – more importantly – the higher the chance of a drive-soothe environment.

One-to-one level: It's one thing for adults to read and digest the ideas in this book; the likelihood is that they'll be able to engage with it at least at some level. A child might not be in such a position. Of course, in the case of Matthew (above), given that he was older, I needed to tread carefully so as not to patronise. But there is still a role around helping young people to understand their thoughts, emotions and feelings.

Sometimes, just acknowledging emotions of frustration – and asking students how they're feeling – can be a useful way to defuse, unpick and calm. Essentially, I think we're asking to connect with students on a human level to help them 'come down' if they feel emotional extremes. Let's imagine you've kept a student back for poor behaviour, or you're having a one-to-one discussion in class – even just 'standing outside' of the situation can be incredibly powerful to defuse. You might ask 'What's going on, then?' (as if to assume that this kind of choice is really unlike them, and let them know that you're still on their side) or you could ask 'What's happened? I'm surprised because...'.

There's no question in my mind that being aware and noticing emotions and feelings is powerful to say the least. Things like the Anger Iceberg[43] and Blob Trees[44] can be incredibly powerful tools to promote emotional literacy. Again, it's all about defusion and separating thoughts from emotions and feelings. If nothing else, they are an exceptionally useful place to begin a conversation.

One particularly interesting area of study is the mapping of emotions onto physical areas of the body by Lauri Nummenmaa and her colleagues,[45] who examined the link between emotions and the physical sensations we feel in our bodies. By asking people to colour in silhouettes where they felt increasing or decreasing sensitivity in their own bodies as a response to images, words, stories and facial expressions, they concluded that irrespective of culture, patterns emerged in terms of how we experience emotions on a physical level. In other words, our physical feelings can actually drive emotions to the surface so we can make sense of what's going on.

43. Benson, K. (2016) 'The anger iceberg', *The Gottman Institute* [blog]. Available at: www.bit.ly/2GmrVb7 (Accessed 15 Oct 2018).
44. www.bit.ly/2IaOj9a (Accessed 15 Oct 2018).
45. Nummenmaa, L., Glerean, E., Hari, R. and Hietanen, J. K. (2014) 'Bodily maps of emotions', *Proceedings of the National Academy of Sciences* 111 (2) pp. 646–651.

I wonder if we might start to ask students to reflect on what's happening for them physically when they are experiencing intense emotion. Fundamentally, we need to provide a platform to help students separate their experience – from the psychological to the physical. By doing so, we are giving them the space to understand and make sense of their feelings in a way that is sustainable in the longer term as well. At the risk of repeating myself, it's about breaking the loop between thoughts, feelings, emotions and behaviours. Not long ago, I remember hearing a phenomenal – and I do mean *phenomenal* – thump in the classroom above me when I was teaching. A young boy had overturned a desk after being annoyed that a supply teacher had told him off. I had to investigate (I wasn't teaching at the time – I was sitting marking). I found the boy – a gibbering wreck sat on the nearby stairs. We chatted about how he was feeling, and we just unpicked the difference between the thought ('This is unfair'), the emotion ('I'm pissed off'), the feeling ('I'm sick of the unfairness here') and the behaviour ('I'm going to tip the table'). It worked to the extent that he was able to go back and apologise before his year manager came and was able to have the situation explained and placed into context. He would be sanctioned for his *behaviour* – not for being *him*. As far as I'm concerned, if we can help children to separate and understand the difference between their insides and their outsides (in terms of behavioural choices), then that's the start.

To varying degrees, asking students to focus on the links between thoughts, feelings and behaviours is incredibly important. As I've touched on above, whether we like it or not, our brains make sense out of things in all kinds of ways. For students, that can mean 'Oh, it's *this* subject, I'm always rubbish in here, I've got nothing to lose, so I'll keep that going.' In a funny kind of way, that predictability can be comforting and familiar for them; it's up to us to help them unpick this. For me, the bottom line is clear, and it is empowering: *humans aren't special*. We have genetic influences, environmental influences, and triggers which might be completely out of our control. But I come back to Paul Gilbert: it's not our fault – or our students' fault – but it *is* our responsibility.

Key points:

- The most important relationship you have is with yourself.
- Being able to see yourself as an individual within a much bigger picture is key to gaining perspective.
- Developing your inner compassionate voice and noticing your own thoughts, emotions, feelings and behaviours is not a quick fix, but it does lessen the intensity of negative experiences.
- A key to all relationships is unpicking narratives (stories we might tell ourselves to make sense of the world).
- Compassion has its inhibitors, and it's important to recognise those; in essence, when we are frustrated or dislike ourselves or others, it's harder to use a compassionate voice. Awareness and practice are essential.
- You can begin to plan for difficult situations by thinking of others as humans first, and separating behaviours from the underlying causes.
- We need to build the language of understanding around mental health – especially for young people.
- Providing a platform for emotional literacy is important for young people because it can help them to understand and articulate their thoughts, emotions, feelings and behaviours.

Section 4: Compassionate teaching

A. Compassionate planning: why we need to listen to science

B. Teaching with compassion

C. A compassionate approach to marking

In recent years, alongside the faux-liberal obsessions with targets and measurability, there has also been a shift in research which has given us new insights into the mechanisms of learning, and how we can best direct our time and resources. In light of what's been discussed in the book to this point, it's important to reflect upon some of the strategies that speak directly to a compassionate framing of teaching – for both students and teachers. This is about work-life balance as well as being as effective as possible.

You may well have come across some of these concepts and ideas, but it's important to synthesise and reimagine some of this stuff through a compassionate lens. There are two guiding principles:

1. *Honesty* – including where your students are in their learning, as well as your own learning in terms of subject knowledge.

2. *Warmth* – remembering that learning is complex and fluid, and that ultimately all we can ask of ourselves is to be reflective.

I don't want to go into huge amounts of depth across loads of different subjects (many of the examples will be English as that is my area); the point is to provide enough of an indication to know how to go and do it (I'll show you where you can go to find more out too). Importantly, though, the methods discussed here are a way of minimising threat and ensuring clarity and transparency about what is happening in your classroom (promoting soothe and drive, hopefully). By definition, students must encounter some kind of unfamiliarity if learning is to happen – we are in the business of framing it in the best way possible. What we need to do is encourage risk-taking and the acceptance of failing (without being 'failures' – important distinction). This is where *thinking* happens. This is when *learning* happens.

I'm going to start with how we can take ownership of what we want our students to know, before looking at how we can triangulate this within the classroom and our continual monitoring of this through our marking. I'd say that these three elements need to be in constant dialogue – and in the process they will ease our burden in terms of workload. You won't always need to pore over every book all of the time if you know what you're looking for; and you don't need to differentiate a million different resources if your culture and direction are aligned. In essence, a thoroughly thought-through long-term plan ought to cut the need for us to be wandering all over the place, scrambling to cover the right things as we teach. In turn, a well-pitched lesson with the best explanations and questions can help us to more accurately feed back to our students, because we'll have a much clearer vision in terms of what we are looking for in the students' work, and how our teaching is manifesting in their work. Finally, to complete the cycle (and begin it again), a greater purpose in terms of our approach to marking will be explored as the key to reducing workload.

A. Compassionate planning: why we need to listen to science

'People are naturally curious, but they are not naturally good thinkers; unless the cognitive conditions are right, people will avoid thinking'
Daniel Willingham

It's striking how modern evidence-based approaches ask us to be truly empathetic to our students and their experiences. The central component to our current understanding of learning is the interplay between long-term and working memory; meeting someone and finding out their name is Kevin is different knowledge to, say, your knowledge of the other really annoying Kevin you remember from university that has coloured your experiences of all the Kevins you've met since. The key to our students' thinking – and learning – is getting long-term and working memory to interact. Learning only happens when long-term memory is *altered*. Peps Mccrea puts it well when he says we need to think about how the working memory *executes* what's in the long-term memory. Ultimately, threat-based strategies such as avoidance of failure and exam focus are not a sustainable means of getting this to happen – they'll lead to burnout and poor motivation eventually. If you are asking these two systems to talk to each other whilst asking your brain to worry about the consequences if it goes wrong, not only is the motivation unsustainable, but the conditions for genuine thinking to happen are less than optimal.

Creating (just about the right kind) of inefficiencies

I've just recently signed up with a personal trainer. He has me doing things which feel bloody impossible. What I've noticed is that to avoid pain or strain, our bodies – well, *my* body – cheats. It'll do anything to avoid pushing itself in a way which might hurt. I look like a beached whale writhing about on his garage floor; he must think it's hilarious. But to get fitter and stronger, we need to be encouraged to push beyond our limits. (He's nice, by the way; he doesn't shout at me like a drill sergeant. See Section 3 for a rationale of why I think this works best.) The brain is the same: it kind of cheats.

Much of what we do every day isn't new to us, per se: it's basically a variation on things we've done before. Take driving, for example. Willingham compares the mental strain on a learner driver compared to an experienced one. It's a different ball game entirely. In other words, thinking is *hard work*, hence the reason our relationship with it is, shall we say, complex. What we need to do is create the conditions whereby as much 'discomfort' or 'uncertainty' can be tolerated without it becoming threatening. This is what Mary Myatt refers to in the title of her book *High Challenge, Low Threat*. Below is Willingham's model of the mind. It's remarkably simple.

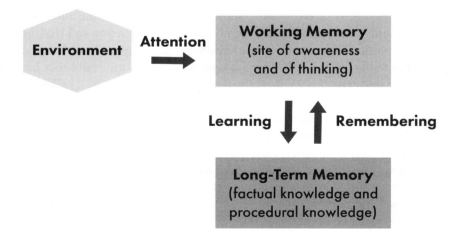

Although we like finding things out, Willingham also observes that 'curiosity is fragile'. (That's one way of putting it – anyone who taught my Year 11s a couple of years back will testify to that particular little nugget.) So, a word search consisting of nine letters or a beginner's Sudoku puzzle are likely to become laborious and unstimulating due to a lack of challenge, just as rocking up to a Harvard University lecture on neuroscience half way through a semester is likely to become impossible to follow very quickly (in fairness, for me, so will nipping up the corridor to Dr Ferguson's Year 8 Chemistry lesson).

A driving reason why curiosity is so fragile is due to cognitive load on our working memory, which is basically a way of saying how much strain we're putting on the brain to comprehend something. Cognitive load can either be *intrinsic* – owing to the complexity of the information (2×20 is a little less difficult to process than, say, standard deviation because it needs fewer steps and information in order for it to be understood) – or *extrinsic* – owing to factors in the tasks we set that need thought but aren't actually part of the learning. The latter refers to instructions as well as content: from the point of view of a student, they won't be able to process a whiteboard full of, say, ten instructions or things to remember in a task. We can't *hold* that much information in our mind at once, let alone use it as a framework to be practising a new skill within. To be compassionate to the students in front of us, there are two golden rules:

1. **Understand the *intrinsic* complexity of what we're asking them to do.** Place yourself in the shoes of someone doing whatever you're asking for the first time. Start from scratch in your mind and think through the steps. 99% of the time it's much harder than we assume: we're professionals with stacks of experience and/ or qualifications; we have schemas and knowledge in our minds honed through years of practise. Students don't.

2. **Eliminate as much *extrinsic* load as possible.** Steve Jobs famously used to have strict limits on his presentation slides for a reason. Too much text? Chop it down. Instructions? No more than three at once as a rule of thumb. Also, can you turn lengthier explanations into diagrams or concrete analogies? Think of this like Ockham's razor – well, more like Ockham's guillotine: be brutal and strict.

Taking ownership of knowledge: breaking the ice between long-term and working memory

In Willingham's model above, I feel like 'environment' really means 'context', including prior motivations, experience, teacher and peer relationships – and so it goes on. We can't guarantee anything, obviously, but we can stack the odds in our favour. As well as the things discussed in Section 3, we can also think about our pedagogy and subject knowledge, which – taken together – are our best hope of breaking the ice between long-term and working memory.

We should be planning for long-term and working memory in our classrooms. Senior and middle leaders are obviously the key drivers in any school, but we can seize control in our immediate contexts. In the not-too-distant past, most schools tended to rotate their schemes of work on half-termly cycles, resulting in a summative assessment that was marked, taken down, and fed into a central system as a concrete measure of progress. Revisiting didn't really happen, so consolidation wasn't given a chance. Given the complexities of measuring progress and the distinction between progress and attainment, this was a remarkably over-simplified structure.[46] The solution? We should start by putting ourselves in the students' shoes: what are they experiencing in your subject's curriculum (as well as others – more for senior leaders)? What knowledge and skills are they being exposed to? When and how often does revisiting happen?

Increasing numbers of teachers are now aware of the 'forgetting curve'[47] which allows us to see the importance of recall in order to build long-term memory. The key is to take real ownership of what is being taught at every level of the curriculum. By this, I mean *really* think about what we want our students to know and do, and why. What I don't mean is continual

---

46. For explanations, see:
• Sherrington, T. (2018) 'How can we measure and report progress meaningfully?', *Teacherhead* [blog]. Available at: www.bit.ly/2N2mvmd (Accessed 15 Oct 2018).
• Benyohai, M. (2018) 'The difference between measuring progress and attainment', *Medium.com*. Available at: www.bit.ly/2N1SaUA (Accessed 15 Oct 2018).
47. www.bit.ly/2N1T5Ew

practice on the end thing (i.e. death by summative assessment). Matthew Syed's wonderful book *Bounce* seems to have been misinterpreted by some as claiming that throwing the same thing at students time and time again will somehow (perhaps by osmosis!) lead them to master the skills to achieve – without doing anything in the middle to effect change. Here, I'll start by thinking about units of work, and then look at what happens in individual lessons, and then reflect on marking.

Compassionate schemes of work

A 'lesson' needs to be seen as a chance to continually revisit and enhance long-term memory. By this token, a scheme of work (or whatever you want to call it) cannot be entirely divorced from the units around it either. This isn't about being robotic; it's about being aware of our direction of travel – and that of our students.

One thing I'd really like to point out here is that planning in this way will genuinely ease the burden throughout the teaching sequence. It takes the pressure off in terms of content coverage, and it should steer us in the right direction, while still giving us the ability to explore a whole range of (relevant) possibilities throughout the lessons. A 'compassionate' scheme of work should:

1. **Clearly outline (and pre-set) the assessment and mark scheme to give us the best chance of understanding progress of the students.** Sadly, learning isn't intrinsically appealing all of the time; we need an end point and something to aim for, and it's important that students and teachers understand what this is. Note the link to Mary Welford's ideas about consistency and clarity being a marker of *kindness*.

2. **Include a 'Big Picture' slide.** The slide doesn't need to be hugely detailed or even beautifully designed(!); it just needs to outline the topic, what we are working towards, and the driving questions we will be addressing each week. It just helps to contextualise what's going on.

3. **Outline the threshold concepts that will underpin the knowledge (and be clear with yourself about when you will revisit them**

explicitly). According to Jan Meyer and Ray Land,[48] a threshold concept 'represents a transformed way of understanding, or interpreting, or viewing something without which the learner cannot progress'. They even call it 'troublesome knowledge' as it might disrupt and unpick an often comfortable understanding of the world. So, we can't expect students to learn simple facts in no particular order and magically do well; we must ask what has to come first to establish the grounds for meaningful shifts in their understanding. More than anything, it's about really getting to grips with the big ideas that should be underpinning the learning. The example I've used below is *Macbeth*: I'd argue that you cannot really begin to engage with the text meaningfully until you have a thorough understanding of the wider context and language structures which need to be explored explicitly to really unpick it. David Didau has blogged wonderfully about this too.[49]

4. **Outline the knowledge that the students will need in order to move forward.** In *Battle Hymn of the Tiger Teachers: The Michaela Way*,[50] Katharine Birbalsingh's introduction beautifully argues for the re-emergence of knowledge at the heart of everything we do. Initially, it was hard for me to get my head around this, but in the time I've embraced 'knowledge' – including my own – it's made a real difference. Unless we make the knowledge *explicit,* trying to make learning happen is like trying to run a car without fuel, or building a house without a foundation – it's not only counterintuitive; it's nigh on *impossible.*

5. **List the vocabulary that will help to structure and scaffold the knowledge.** Alex Quigley's incredible *Closing the Vocabulary*

48. Flanagan, M. (2018) 'Threshold concepts: undergraduate teaching, postgraduate training, professional development and school education', *Michael Thomas Flanagan's Home Page* [Online]. Available at: www.bit.ly/2E9lXYM (Accessed 20 Oct 2018).

49. Didau, D. (2015) 'Using threshold concepts to design a KS4 English curriculum', *Learning Spy* [Online]. Available at: www.bit.ly/2WTjIjA (Accessed 20 Oct 2018).

50. Birbalsingh, K. (2016) *Battle Hymn of the Tiger Teachers.* Woodbridge: John Catt Educational Ltd.

Gap[51] has successfully drawn attention to the power of vocabulary to drive learning. Not only does it drive learning, but it provides students with tangible hooks upon which to hang their knowledge. One distinction that I have found incredibly useful is the one between Tier 1, 2 and 3 vocabulary.[52] Tier 1 vocabulary is the stuff we hear all the time in everyday use; but Tier 2 comprises the type of words most closely linked to academia – the type of words those from 'word-poor' backgrounds don't necessarily encounter as often. Tier 3 is subject-specific vocabulary that is not necessarily relevant to other subjects.

6. **List the sequence in which students will encounter content.** Many schemes of work have often been limited to variations of this alone. It's important, of course, but really only in the context of the other stuff. I always find it useful to have a driving question every week. It was suggested to me that this should be seen in every lesson, which I really like as well – it helps to give purpose to what's going on. Each week has a question, but you could also drill down into individual lessons too and have a question to frame what's going on. I much prefer this to learning objectives as this harnesses curiosity in my view.

I think this is compassionate on the grounds that it requires *us* to be honest and transparent with ourselves about what's needed – including enhancing our own subject knowledge – and how the learning is going to be driven. In the process, our students will be under no illusions about this either. An example scheme outline and big picture slide are on the next two pages.

---

51. Quigley, A. (2018) *Closing the vocabulary gap*. Abingdon: Routledge.
52. Didau, D. (2014) 'Closing the language gap: building vocabulary', *Learning Spy* [Online]. Available at: www.bit.ly/2tjG4x1 (Accessed 20 Oct 2018).

Unit title: *Macbeth: an examination of human agency*

Summative assessment: Paper 1 extract and thematic question – Act 1 Scene iii, 'The evil inside?'

Sequencing of content	Content coverage	Driving questions	Threshold concept addressed	Links to previous learning NB: left blank as this is dependent on the wider curriculum	Tier 2 Vocabulary
Sequence 1:	A1S1–4	Where does evil come from?	EA, N		ambitious, callous, conniving, malicious, courageous, moral, ambiguous, convoluted, inevitable
Sequence 2:	A1S5–A2S4	What causes Macbeth to commit the ultimate crime?	EA, T		**Tier 3 Vocabulary**
Sequence 3:	A3S1–A4S3	How does Shakespeare demonstrate Macbeth's metamorphosis?	T, NS, L		hamartia, peripeteia, and anagnorisis, catharsis, Divine Right of Kings, soliloquy, hubris, iambic pentameter, dramatic irony
Sequence 4:	A5S1–A5S7	What does Shakespeare reveal about the consequences of evil?	T, NS, L		
Sequence 5:	A5S8–A5S9	Was Macbeth destined to die?	T, NS, L		
Sequence 6:	Whole play	What can the story teach us about our own lives?	EA, L		

Threshold concepts: Elizabethan Audiences (EA), Elements of Tragedy (T), Narrative Structure (N), Language Structure (L). **NB: these are the kinds of concepts we can design when we look at a curriculum as a whole across all year groups**

Macbeth: an examination of human agency

Overarching Question:
What does Shakespeare reveal about human agency through Macbeth?

Our Assessment:
16th December - a question just like the one you'll get in a real exam.

How we're going to visit the text:
1. Where does evil come from? A1S1-4 (Also the overall plot)
2. What causes Macbeth to commit the ultimate crime? A1S5-A2S4
3. How does Shakespeare demonstrate Macbeth's metamorphosis? A3S1-A4S3
4. What does Shakespeare reveal about the consequences of evil? A5S1-A5S7
5. Was Macbeth destined to die? A5S8-A5S9
6. What can the story teach us about our own lives?

We need to be aware of:
- What the story meant to his audience
- What makes this a true tragedy?
- The structure of the story
- The structure of the language

The strength of planning in this way drives us to take ownership of the knowledge that the students need over the longer term, and also really ensures that we ground ourselves each time we teach in terms of the bigger picture. In other words, we don't just 'do' lessons, but we are moving forwards, with knowledge as the driver of skills. The threshold concepts are the 'We need to be aware of' in terms of those aspects of the topic that will need to be understood in order to really unlock the topic. These are things that, in different guises and throughout the story, are revisited and need to be understood as transcending the topic. Again, this isn't groundbreaking; it's just about being clear on what *you* know and what you want the *students* to know.

Linked to the 'ownership of knowledge' idea, as an English specialist, one thing I did for literature was to create knowledge books. They included:

1. Pre-agreed key scenes/moments from the texts
2. Quotes with words blanked out to learn
3. '20 to know' short-answer questions (with answers) for parents to be testing them on

4. Key quotes (thematically organised) and knowledge organisers with Tier 2 and 3 vocabulary

Yes, it took time; but my goodness did it pay me back during term time as we moved through a core text, for example. It also 'outsourced' my own planning to an extent as I had a structure to follow. Students just had to open the right page and have all of their notes in front of them – notes that they would add to as they moved along (rather than random exercise book pages that they'd probably not go back to). Again, to paraphrase Mccrea, I outsourced the knowledge to one easily accessible place for easy retrieval whenever appropriate.

As part of the planning, Tier 2 and 3 vocabulary is absolutely fundamental. I previously didn't understand vocabulary or really recognise its significance; thanks primarily to Alex Quigley and David Didau, I do now. Now, I try to think of a unit of work as a building, with the weekly sequences as the frame of the house and the Tier 2 and 3 vocabulary at the foundations, allowing the students to explore the content and concepts, but complete the furnishings with their own meaning (I'm sorry, I know it sounds incredibly naff). This may be different for other subjects that are perhaps more objective (a student's individual take on *A Christmas Carol* leaves more room for interpretation than the periodic table).

B. Teaching with compassion

'I have just three things to teach: simplicity, patience, compassion. These three are your greatest treasures.'

Lao Tzu

What follows is an explanation of how the above can feed into individual lessons. In other words, how do you get long-term and working memory to talk to each other day in, day out?

The role of recap

Just as noticing our mood periodically strengthens our ability to gain perspective, routinely revisiting knowledge and understanding our journey as teachers and learners works much the same way. Debate about engagement and its role in learning is quite fierce, and I don't want to get into it here. However, initiatives like the '5-a-day' ones on #EduTwitter really illustrate how we can try to capture that sense of intrinsic enjoyment through asking students to revisit what they've learned through short-answer questions. It's amazing how much students love a quiz (seriously). The concept is remarkably simple: you begin lessons by asking students five simple questions to recap previous learning. For example, if you have five short-answer questions on the board as a 'do now' task, you also have a free opportunity to throw in a question to test something from a previous unit which can be linked to what's happening in the current unit. Psychologically, it's 'safe': it's low-stakes and speaks to curiosity because there's not really any significant threat to not getting it right. And anyway, the important aspect to this is the process of trying to *retrieve* from the long-term memory. There's all kinds of ways you can do this:

1. One-word/short-answer questions

2. Multiple-choice questions

3. This is the answer; what is the question?

4. Crosswords

5. Cloze exercises

6. Find links between terms – place, say, ten words on the board and ask the students to explain five connections

Stripping it back: using a continuum and minimising working memory strain

In terms of what to actually plan into lessons, it's important to be fully aware of the implications of what you are asking students to do. Peps Mccrea's book *Memorable Teaching* is a masterpiece in helping us to minimise working memory strain. He offers nine principles to help us keep things as optimal as possible. Again, ownership over what we want our students to know is fundamental, and it's not as simple as we might assume. For us, launching generally into a topic and exploring it might feel comfortable, because it's familiar; to a student, there's all kinds of unlearned concepts that are just frankly confusing if you're unfamiliar with them. When I worked at my first school, they took a lot of inspiration from the line 'do the project first' in order to really get a grasp of what we want our students to be able to command. The end result – the summative assessment – is the tip of the iceberg, and we've got to keep everything underneath it as lean as possible. So, starting from back to front has genuinely compassionate roots:

End product The final piece we're aiming for	Performance indicators The things a successful piece will contain. For me, this is what bridges knowledge and skill – *what does the 'skill' look like in practice?*	Ideas and opinions Though perhaps not always necessary in every subject, discussing and forming views on the content is an important means of taking ownership	Knowledge and facts The hard content that is needed in order to begin to engage with the topic
An essay on population growth	Evaluative verbs: emphasises, underscores, signifies, symbolises. Grammatical structures, including: complex, compound, colons, semi colons	Moral considerations, possible solutions	Forces behind it, issues linked, statistics, sustainability, keywords Exam question appearance Specification requirements

I like the analogy of owning knowledge being akin to stripping back a car engine – in other words, really seeing the component parts and how they can come together to create the end product. Unless the learner understands how those component parts work together, they will run into difficulty extremely easily when they're on their own (who hasn't heard the classic 'I don't know how to start it' before?). Learning isn't linear. We can't spend a lesson on knowledge and then assume it's done and dusted, obviously; but when we focus on whatever our performance indicators are, we can provide the students with a knowledge organiser or a list of key facts to allow them to focus on the thing they are perfecting in that moment. (Again, see Mccrea's idea of 'outsourcing'.) In other words: 'Don't worry about holding that thing in your head while you focus on this thing. We can bring it together later.' One last point on this: there is absolutely no assumption from my part here about the order of these things. Once you unpack the complexity of what you want the students to do, it's a case of reflecting on the sequence in which you think this should be delivered and processed in. Neither – by the way – is there any assumption that this works the same in every subject; but I just think there's a need for picking apart knowledge, skills and application, and being honest and open about it.

This continuum is probably one of the biggest threshold concepts I've learned as a teacher; it's something I wish I'd discovered years ago. Previously, I'd plough through a topic, then bung a few sentence openers on the board; the students would complete them and I'd take that performance as poor evidence of their learning. What we are doing by noticing this is easing the burden on the students, and giving them the space to grow. After all, it is a lot to ask students to write an essay on population growth, paying attention to a new grammatical structure (e.g. a colon to clarify a point they are making) alongside an opinion they might be trying to communicate.

Bread and butter: explanations and questions

For me, the best explanations of teaching are the ones that recognise the balance between craft and science. Andy Tharby's recent book *How To Explain Absolutely Anything to Absolutely Anyone*[53] is a masterpiece in this respect, by the way. I would say that being human and being ready to give links to personal stories, analogies, metaphor and real-life tangible examples is incredibly important. The analogy of an iPhone X vs XS is always useful to explain subtle improvements in upgrading vocabulary; I've also previously relayed the analogy of my little boy's doctor – when he was in hospital, his doctor went through an evaluation process before diagnosing him to explain her reasons (e.g. the last time he ate; if he'd been sick; whether he had shown symptoms before; etc.). Also, demonstrating processes or concepts physically or through diagrams is a wonderful way of making what is implicit more explicit. I am reliably informed that osmosis can be explained through the use of a grape and a raisin (demonstrating the physical transfer of water to show the

---

53. Tharby, A. (2018) *How to explain absolutely anything to absolutely anyone.* Carmarthen: Crown House Publishing Ltd.

difference between the two); or mass through dissolving salt into one of two identical pans of water, and then weighing them. These explicit links and stories can be a real vehicle for change in the minds of the students.

As well as this, there's a real skill to moving between explanations and questions. This is where the explicit teaching of vocabulary can play a role. Being explicit about vocabulary and its link to what you're driving at is vital. Staying with *Macbeth* for a moment, let's imagine we've covered the word 'metamorphosis' in a previous lesson. I might begin the discussion with images on the board of Voldemort, Darth Vader or any other villain who believes in their own hype and who has gone through a change, as well as the words 'hubris', 'callous', 'influence' and 'inevitable', with the following steps planned in my mind:

Me – recap: OK, so can you tell me something about what happens to at least one of these people on the board? I'll give you 20 seconds to think on your own. OK, so, Ben, what do you think?

Ben: They all make bad choices.

Me – clarify: How do you mean? Can you be more specific?

Ben: Well, Vader let himself grow evil with the Dark Side and Voldemort just wanted to live forever and didn't care about anything else.

Me – elaborate: Yes, and they experience a change in their personalities somehow. Another word for that? I'll give you ten seconds here. Habeeba, what word have we looked at that links to change?

Habeeba: Metamorphosis.

Me – deepen: Yes, brilliant. Let's just focus on this for a moment: what or who drives Macbeth's metamorphosis? You should try to link your explanations to the words on the board as well. I'll give you a minute here. OK – Daniel, what are your thoughts? Remember to use the vocabulary if you can.

Daniel: He can't avoid his own hubris, but he is forced into murder by Lady Macbeth who is really selfish and pushes him into it and influences him.

Me – evaluate: OK, yes, that's nice. Tom, do you agree?

Tom: Kind of.

Me – evaluate: Why only kind of?

Tom: Because he is callous by his own choice too. He completely chooses to betray his own king and isn't physically forced into it.

I apologise sincerely if you think this sounds like a script from *The Waltons*, but I hope you understand the point I'm trying to make through it. Questioning is a really important component to drawing out and developing the right kind of culture in a classroom. It's fundamental to question with real purpose, and think: what am I trying to achieve here? At times, I've found myself asking questions for the sake of it, and discussion quickly disappears into the abyss. We could consider questions within the following categories:

Recap	Recall facts and shorter answers to get going. *What is...? When does...? Who...? Remind me of...*
Clarify	Be sure about what a response means – ask the student to be specific about what they've said. *Do you mean...? Just so I'm sure, is this because...?*
Elaborate	Ask for explanations, drivers and reasons. *How does this link to...? Is there a different reason for this? How else is this important?*
Deepen	Try to probe further, and possibly look for alternatives or even a focus on specific pieces of vocabulary. *Go on... Tell me more... What might this tell us?*
Evaluate	Begin to collect thoughts and form an overall response. *To what extent do you agree...? Are you entirely certain about...?*

Again, there is nothing avant-garde here, but I like the idea of recap and hinging the learning onto key vocabulary and previous concepts to support and drive it forward. There's no question in my mind that just having our own sense of clarity about classroom discussions and their purpose can help us to tread that line and respect the fragility of curiosity(!). One thing which I don't think is emphasised enough is giving students the time to think before we expect an answer; more than anything, it removes some of the risk and threat from the situation, and gives some breathing space to think about what you want them to consider. Another thing which can be difficult to stop yourself doing is asking a question then asking it again before the student has even blinked (I speak from experience). It's another very specific area of my teaching I've had to work and reflect on. I've been guilty of questions such as: 'Can you give me an example of a noun? What types of noun are there?' – which question is the poor soul supposed to answer?

Previously, I discussed the idea of creating a positive buzz in the room, bouncing around open-ended questions such as '_____, would you agree?' or '_____, give me a reason why what _____ said might not necessarily be accurate.' Growing an environment where students are comfortable with this kind of thing is a really precious thing, but it takes time, and – most importantly – consistency. The other side of this coin is to model academic discourse here as well. Where possible, it's important to insist on full sentences and celebrate the use of high-level vocabulary. So often, it's self-consciousness that might make this feel a bit uncomfortable at first. But Section 3 discussed uncertainty and discomfort; I hope this is of some use here. We can acknowledge this with the class when we are insisting on full sentences and high levels, and celebrate when they do this to gradually embed that culture. There is a huge difference between blindly 'teaching to the top' and compassionately acknowledging the difficulties of learning. To summarise, then: relentless positivity and knowing where you want to go with a line of questioning are both crucial.

Modelling

Give me modelling over success criteria any day – it's concrete, and a good model can create more meaningful success criteria as a by-product anyway. Success criteria are a good starting place for those who already have a firm grip on what's going on; they're not so good for first-timers, because as a condensed list of what success should be, it assumes all kinds of things, which in a classroom is risky, to say the least. Lots of what's discussed here is outlined in Barak Rosenshine's 'Principles of

Instruction'.[54] Alongside Doug Lemov's *Teach Like a Champion*, and Peps Mccrea's *Memorable Teaching*, I'd say these are the three texts that are the most important to teachers at any level.

One of the things Rosenshine talks about is modelling under the banner of 'scaffolds for difficult tasks'. This speaks directly to the continuum outlined above – it's about being explicit in terms of what you'd like the students to be working on. There's different sorts of modelling – and again, if we put ourselves into the position of the students, we need it to be relevant to our learning experience (no need to show off and smash 100% A level answers out and expect them to pick it up magically). One core principle that transcends any modelling is the craft of unpicking its relevance in terms of moving students on: we always need to ask, 'What are students actually gaining from this example, and how is it going to help them?' Just mentioning a few aspects of it – again I have historically been shocking for this – and then hoping for the best is not enough.

- **The 'what we're aiming for' model.** The most obvious one: pre-prepared, with your take on what the students should be aiming to produce. From this, labelling – *slowly and methodically* – and discussing key features is key. This can include any aspect – knowledge or skill – you want them to be honing. It might be worth collecting examples of work to use in the future as you go along – it's a huge timesaver, by the way. Careful here, though: best cases can lead to undermining confidence if we're not careful.

- **The 'meh' model.** A pedestrian response that students can hack into and pick apart easily. It's not appalling, but nor is it top-drawer stuff. This can be great for building confidence. I like this because students will likely recognise the relevance of the answer and hopefully know how to drive it on.

- **The 'live' model.** I think this is the hardest one to master; here, it's about questioning and building a live example *with* the students. You need to be aware of maintaining positivity and pace whilst concentrating and creating something that isn't just *yours*, but

54. Rosenshine, B. (2012) 'Principles of instruction: research-based strategies that all teachers should know', *American Educator* 36 (1) pp. 12–19, 39. Available at: www.bit.ly/2SxqbSN (Accessed 18 Oct 2018).

representative of the students. If you have an iPad and a decent ICT technician in your school, I'd recommend getting your hands on a *Doceri* licence. It allows you to have visualisation tool in your hand as you move around the room, highlighting, writing and even marking students' work. Failing this, you can just buy a static visualiser that sits on your desk, under which you can place work or texts to annotate 'live'.

- **The 'nearly done' model.** Provide students with an incomplete piece of work at whatever standard you think is needed, which will provide a really useful basis as a platform to launch from. Is the work poor? How can it be improved as we continue? Is it strong? How can we maintain the standard?

- **The 'non' model.** This isn't so much about producing a piece of work as such; it's about pre-empting errors and making a list of them before we start a piece of work. Ask the students what to look out for and what the typical errors a piece of work like this might contain.

Some places call these kinds of things 'me, we, you' to capture the ways in which the students' work is scaffolded. Again, there's a difference between doing things like this because we're 'supposed to' and actually being able to walk in the shoes of the student and really empathise with the difficulties of learning something for the first time. Mindfully noticing the struggles (theirs and yours) and being warm and encouraging is key.

Inconvenient truths: we need to talk about...progress

Harry Fletcher-Wood's excellent book *Responsive Teaching*[55] is right up there with Mccrea's book. His chapter 'How can we tell what students learned in a lesson?' picks apart the idea of students 'looking like' they're learning versus what is *actually* going on. Again, it's about being unwaveringly honest with yourself about what you want the students to *gain* from the lesson. Assessing students' progress is obviously a continual process. Again, it's about being honest with yourself, and not being afraid to stop what's happening. Rosenshine talks about 'obtaining a high success rate' and gives an example of a teacher that realised their students weren't 'getting it', cancelled the homework task that had been

55. Fletcher-Wood, H. (2018) *Responsive teaching*. Abingdon: Routledge.

planned, and retaught the content the next day.[56] We've talked about recap above in a manner that's designed to consciously build knowledge, but we need to think about this in two more ways:

Assessing what's going on *during* the lesson

1. **Hinge questions.** These are questions which help us understand whether we can 'move on' in a lesson. They are fabulous because they allow us to truly reflect where students are in their learning. Whole-class methods involving thumbs up, middle or down are next to useless because we can't truly be sure whether a feeling of confidence is actually the same as mastery of the topic. The focus of hinge questions is misconceptions; we have to be aware of the *misconceptions* that students might have in what they've learned, and ask them to form an answer in a way that demonstrates accuracy. It's not about tricking students, but about asking them to clarify and be clear about what they think. Hinge questions, I think, are more effective when it comes to checking facts rather than subjective interpretation. Students, for example, often find it difficult to distinguish between a content verb (like 'push') and an auxiliary verb (like 'was' or 'is'), so I might ask them to identify the verbs in the following: 'I ran to school'/'I am silly'/'He was running to school'. The key here is the 'I am silly' because there are no content verbs in it. If they've mastered the concept they should be able to explain why 'am' is the verb, and not 'silly' (students will often think of being 'silly' as a verb you can perform). Here, again, you are 'owning' knowledge and pre-empting misconceptions.

2. **Being curious.** It's important to be curious and take an interest in *where* answers came from. I love asking questions like 'What makes you say that?' and 'Can you explain that for me?' Obviously, this links with being relentlessly positive so as not to be activating threat systems; but celebrating curiosity is really important, as is encouraging debate.

3. **Role reversal.** It's been done in various different guises before,

---

56. Rosenshine, B. (2012) 'Principles of instruction: research-based strategies that all teachers should know', *American Educator* 36 (1) pp. 12–19, 39. Available at: www.bit.ly/2SxqbSN (Accessed 18 Oct 2018).

but a model answer can be provided at a time in the lesson after discussions and the 'build-up' to a task has been done. Students can then create their own *specific* success criteria to feed back or to demonstrate their knowledge of the quality of the model. Again, it's about making the implicit *explicit*.

Assessing at the end

1. **Exit tickets.** I unashamedly love these short little tasks we ask students to complete at the end of a lesson. But they can be done poorly; we need to be really clear about what we want them to tell us. Simply giving a multiple-choice question with two ridiculous responses, a mildly relevant answer and an obviously right answer will only tell us that the students can definitely pick out the irrelevant content. In some ways, I think these are a bit like hinge questions at the end of a lesson, and should be designed to 'speak to' misconceptions that may have arisen. A key to these, where possible, is to make them short in nature so you can easily identify the response. Harry Fletcher-Wood discusses dividing (separate piles to show success, partial success, and no success), digging (separating 'partial' and 'no' into piles and looking into what's happened) and 'deciding' in terms of looking at patterns and working through how to move forward.

2. **Tell me why.** Asking students to self and peer assess *explicitly* is really powerful. So often, this kind of thing can lead to no more than a colouring exercise – and a messy one at that. Rather, I like the idea of guiding this more specifically. Try asking students to label specific aspects of the work that they've completed during the lesson – again, it's about being entirely clear with what is being learned and what success should look and feel like. Also, encourage honesty from them; if they're struggling, ask them to write down why, and *at what point* they felt as if they couldn't grasp whatever it was we were asking of them.

A trip across the pond – Cornell note-taking

This, I think, is more easily adapted and useful for older and more able students; but with the right support I really think there's something to this for everyone. It's got a little bit of everything in it: recap, questioning, reflection and spacing. I've used this for A level classes in particular, and it's a fabulous way of ensuring that they revisit what they should be doing between lessons. You can also have variants of this depending on what you're trying to achieve, but the core of this is what we are being extremely clear about: how students can be preparing for lessons and the link between this and their independent study. In other words, it's a note-taking structure as well as a revision structure. Note: you can give students this outline *alongside* an exercise book for them to be summarising and taking away to learn at home. It can be a useful 'self-check' tool.

The outline of the pages on a page of A4 should look like this:

Key words	Key information
Questions	
Summary	

1. **Take notes** in lessons and use subheadings for new topics. Paraphrase and summarise as the lesson is happening.

2. For homework – preferably on the same day – ask students to **formulate questions** to clarify what they've learned. In other words, questions which, when answered, would be the best indicator that they've learned something in the lesson.

3. Students then cover up the notes and use the key words to prompt them into **reciting and explaining the content** out loud. This can be done with someone at home, too.

4. **Summarise** all of the above in the bottom section; bring it together in a couple of sentences. This might take some time to consolidate and pull together, and isn't as simple as you might think.

5. **Review** the notes. Spend an additional 10–20 minutes per week going over and reciting previous notes.

This is remarkably similar to the system that – unbeknownst to me – I used in my A levels. Constant re-visiting and reviewing is crucial to really strengthen what we've learned. Again, part of my own compassionate learning was that I needed to find a way of extrapolating that out for students and giving them the bridge to get there, rather than simply assuming that that's the easy bit.

The role of collaboration

So, as we've established, learning is bloody hard – and that includes our own as well. Daniel Willingham even dedicates a chapter to this in his incredible book *Why Don't Students Like School?* Plenty has been written on deliberate practice elsewhere, too. Again, being specific and clear about what you'd like to practise is key.

Colleagues should play a huge part in your development, as should you in theirs. This, by the way, is another means of building those compassionate relationships based on sharing and honesty that were discussed in the previous section. Being honest and open is crucial: schools might boast an 'open-door policy' but only when it's open in spirit can you really begin to see people beginning to work along the drive-soothe axis. Picking something specific in your practice is really important – not just 'questioning' or 'marking'. What aspect of questioning are you working on? What do you perceive to be your area for development in terms of questioning? Is it picking the right students? Is it timing, pace or something else? I do like the learning to drive analogy: not only is it much less cognitively demanding on us as we gain more experience, but we also pick up bad habits (speaking for myself).

I had a colleague recently who taught across the corridor from me. He is a wonderful teacher. He'd pop in to see me and give me honest, tangible feedback. I trusted him implicitly, and when he came into my room, my spirits lifted – genuinely. This is the kind of atmosphere we need to be establishing in our schools between colleagues. CFT observes the mind's association of lowering our guards and being taken advantage of, and there is certainly something to this in terms of balancing accountability and establishing these kinds of cultures. One thing we know for sure is that what we have currently does *not* work, and that those schools that are succeeding are doing so in spite of the accountability system rather than because of it.

On the back of this, one thing I would recommend is the practice of 'lesson study'.[57] I love it because it really sits well with the compassionate model. It's about identifying areas of practice you want to deliberately get better at, and the process is remarkably simple:

1. **Plan a lesson with a colleague** – it's important that you *both* have ownership so as to increase the drive you are experiencing together. Predict how the students might respond, and pick three case study students for your colleague to pay particular attention to during the lesson.

2. **Colleague observes** – paying attention to the students identified, and potentially doing some student voice during and after.

3. **Meet again** – reflect and replan together, paying special attention to the aspects you've identified.

---

57. Teacher Development Trust (2018) 'What is lesson study?', *Teacher Development Trust*

It's not about measurability; it's about *transparency*. For me, it's too common for someone being observed to feel completely in dark about what is being looked for. Why? What's the big secret? Too much judgement, too little collaboration, I'm afraid. Looking at this more logistically, there's also a real need to collaborate on the knowledge we as teams want our students to encounter across units of work. Identifying areas of strength not only builds teams, but more strategically taps into the very best knowledge we can give to our students. Variability in knowledge across teams should be embraced: it's time we started taking ownership over our subjects within teams as well as within our classrooms. When I spoke to Dame Alison Peacock, she spoke about not assuming deficit, but looking at what can proactively be *given* to develop others.

C. A compassionate approach to marking

'Compassion is passion with a heart.'
Anonymous

This is one of the areas that tends to provoke anxiety in teachers. Much of this comes from schools' marking policies and their demands on time. In truth, if schools are doing things because it's 'what Ofsted want to see', then they're telling porkies – see for yourself (taken from the Ofsted website):

'Ofsted recognises that marking and feedback to pupils, both written and oral, are important aspects of assessment. However, Ofsted does not expect to see any specific frequency, type or volume of marking and feedback; these are for the school to decide through its assessment policy. Marking and feedback should be consistent with that policy, which may cater for different subjects and different age groups of pupils in different ways, in order to be effective and efficient in promoting learning.'[58]

Thankfully, some of the more extreme policies such as 'triple marking' seem to have died a death in more recent times, but there's still much we can do ourselves to maintain effective but manageable workloads from this perspective. I don't want to labour the idea of compassion at every

---

58. Ofsted (2018) *Ofsted inspections: myths*. Department for Education. Available at: www.bit.ly/2EbWjTn (Accessed 18 Oct 2018).

angle. Rather, as I've mentioned previously, it's about using the concept to pay attention to what's right for you and your students, and keeping it manageable. I will labour the point about *honesty* with oneself, though!

Know *why* you're marking

This is undoubtedly one of those things that you get better at as you go along, but I think it's really important to have a purpose behind our marking. I think one of the fundamentals behind all teacher training needs to be the importance of that cycle of 'plan, mark, teach'. Marking is expensive and time-consuming; we don't need to add 'ineffective' into that horrible mix as well. The golden rule of marking – without a shadow of a doubt – is to *always* know *why* you are sitting down to mark a set of books. In terms of threat, simply 'because someone might be checking' is not going to serve any real purpose, and anyone with any degree of credibility will know the difference between marking for the sake of it and for the sake of meaningful dialogue between student and teacher. I do acknowledge the reality of this, but there needs to be a greater emphasis on the 'drive' element of our motivation systems when marking. By this, I mean it should feel meaningful. If it doesn't, ask yourself *why*.

For me, to help it feel purposeful, there are different reasons to mark:

- To check how the students have responded to the input and the lesson (see the continuum above)
- To give you the chance to direct attention and focus of the students for areas of development
- To help you plan subsequent lessons
- To check for literacy errors – both individual and class patterns
- To give you a chance to praise or intercept in terms of student effort
- To let the students know you take their work seriously
- To give a summative grade and an evaluation of performance

If you think about which of the above are suggestive of lengthier comments from us, it's only really the final bullet point. If we mark books to support progress, then, it makes very little sense to always force ourselves to make lengthy comments.

Minimise time, maximise impact

Something which unites all of what you will read below is maximising the opportunity for students to develop their self-regulation. We want them to respond to feedback, but it needs to be as independently as possible. These strategies are a means of removing the emphasis from teachers and handing autonomy back to students.

Golden rule: always ask students to hand their books in *open* at the relevant page – it saves masses of time.

Golden rule: cut up strips of lined paper to glue into the margins over already completed work – students can simply re-draft over the top.

Golden rule: feedback should *always* be specific and actionable – if they can't *do* something with it (whether it be responding to a question, or a task, or re-practising) then it's hard for them to feel or show that they can move on.

Golden rule: feedback is not about being friendly – although praise can be useful to recognise effort and improvement, we can show the students how much we care in our other behaviours.

Method 1: Use letters/numbers

1. As you read the books, think about the area of development of each student.

2. On a separate piece of paper, write down the area for development (just use your own words) – e.g. 'show more evidence of evaluation', 'essay structure is lacking in direction' – with a number next to it

3. Write just the number down at the bottom of the piece of work.

4. Repeat, re-using numbers if you see the same things reoccur, or adding new ones.

5. You can then design short-response tasks or provide simple instructions for each of the areas of development which the students can complete at the opening of the lesson, or as the first main activity.

Method 2: Dots

This is more of a front-loading activity, but again, the payoff for workload reduction in the long-term is significant. Raid your department stock cupboard for cardboard wallets, and maybe splash out on some coloured sticky dots. Start with, say, ten generic activities that can be placed into the folders and pinned to a wall. You can use them similarly to the method above, but whenever you need, you can just place the right sticky dot into the book for the student to go and get the corresponding resource (this works even more nicely if you have worked out your threshold concepts as a department – maybe the creation of activities and support sheets can be shared across teams).

Method 3: Whole-class feedback

If you search online for 'whole-class feedback templates', you'll be able to find plenty – and all kinds of different variations. The key here is to again minimise the amount you write in books, but spend the time actually *reading* the work of the students, and accumulating worthwhile responses in your own mind. Extrinsic measures can demand a sea of red/green teacher comments; actually, we should spend our time doing our job – not having to *pretend* we are doing it. It's more about your *own* thinking and forward planning than anything else. What's important to note here is that students will know you're reading their work without you always needing to write a comment.

Method 4: Search and rescue

As you read the students' books, use a highlighter to draw attention to a small number of 'fixes' that need to be made when the students redraft their work (see the 'strips of paper' golden rule above). If you want to give them a hint, you could have some up on the board with a list of the possible errors they need to address.

Method 5: Student-friendly grids

Another front-loader in terms of time invested at the start. Based on the criteria you might set out on a piece of work (or even agreed with the class), create a table of simple and actionable generic targets (including space for 'other' for outliers) that you simply highlight and place into the books. If an aspect of the criteria has not been met, then the corresponding column could have a follow-up task. Below is one worked example:

Success Criteria	:-)	:-/	:-(	Follow-up task
Use colons to clarify a point you are making				1. Insert the missing colon into these sentences: Bad memories are like noses everyone's got one. There is only one way we can improve this situation by listening. One word encapsulates how we should feel about this disgusted. 2. Now, choose a place in your work where you feel you need to impactfully make a point, and add in your own sentence using a colon.

One final thought

I've lost count of the number of articles and blog posts I've read that promise to cut marking in half, and then proceed to offer up minor variations on the things I've already done. (My sincere apologies if you feel like this after reading the above.) Sorry to say, but it's not possible to kill marking load totally. The key is to see it as part of a much wider process of planning and teaching. Once we understand that marking is a *part* of the process which can have variations and does not always need to be a long comment in every student's book, then two things happen: the load lessens physically because you realise it's unnecessary; but also whenever you sit down to mark, you are doing so with drive and purpose, making it entirely more meaningful – and *much* less of a grind.

Key points:

- There is nothing avant-garde about teaching with compassion: the fundamental principles, though, are honesty and warmth.
- The interplay between long-term and working memory is key to learning.

- Learning only occurs when long-term memory is altered.
- Understanding cognitive load is essential to minimising strain on working memory.
- Cognitive load can be either intrinsic (task complexity) or extrinsic (unnecessary complications).
- A key component to compassionate teaching is ownership or knowledge and clarity about how we want students to execute that knowledge.
- Longer units of work should be thoroughly thought through in advance, considering the knowledge as it would appear when encountered for the first time by a novice.
- Marking is far too big a deal in teachers' lives. If we begin to see it as part of a cycle, and understand why we are marking when we sit down to mark, we can minimise the threat it poses as well as the time it takes.
- Different forms of feedback can promote our own time management as well as students' ownership of their learning.

Section 5:
The future: reclamation

A. Reframe and reclaim

B. Listening schools

C. What I hope you'll take away from this book

Writing this book has been a privilege. On one level, it's been cathartic, giving me the space to think about my own experiences and find out a little more about my own thoughts. The level of insight I feel that's been achieved would not have been possible, however, without speaking to such a diverse range of colleagues. The issues that face us as a profession are incontrovertible; these are issues that require something from all of us if they are to be addressed. A common theme runs through my research, interviews and my thoughts: reclamation.

A. Reframe and reclaim

'It is no measure of health to be well adjusted to a profoundly sick society.'
Jiddu Krishnamurti

Why reclamation? Because outcome-driven culture – the inception of which was in the name of liberty and equality – has been warped into Frankenstein's monster. Extrinsic measures are used to provide frameworks and indicators to the extent that they have come to define our entire experience of schools. Pitting schools against one another leads to the hoisting of banners on school fences, and more barriers between schools as they are forced into a race to the top. Not only does this contravene what research (alongside our own experience) tells us, but if you try to reconcile this with the literature around mental health, on a much more sinister level it is unquestionably doing us profound harm. Whilst it might be sweeping to say we should abolish all league tables, I think we need to look at what they measure, and what they place value upon. Equally damaging is the insidious – and inevitably long-term – influence of the behaviours that the current educational framework is encouraging. Frankly, I don't care if this is inadvertent or not; it's irresponsible. The unscrupulous behaviours of some individuals you'll have seen hinted at in this book are a response to our cultures and systems. I'd say education in this country is seeing outcomes – in every sense of the word – that are entirely in line with the quality of its systems. Those outcomes are rife with injustice and inequality. This is not what the young people of this country deserve. And it's time we faced up to that fact.

First of all, in the broadest possible sense, education in the UK needs to work out its core purpose and be honest and unashamed about pursuing that purpose because – at the moment – while we're doing a lot of things, we're doing them badly. Systems and structures should exist to provide a minimum standard of service for their end users. We are failing in this respect, and I am absolutely convinced that the best schools in this country succeed *in spite of* – rather than *because of* – the systems underpinning them. I fear that this won't happen until education is moved away from the political agenda. Elections are held every five years and it probably takes about that long for cultural shifts at an organisational level, so the maths doesn't make sense (even before we get into the mathematics and injustice of the dishing-out of examination grades).

Of course, this book has hopefully given you a chance to reflect upon how you can reclaim your own profession in your own context. Compassion is about honesty. Some of the things you will ask yourself about your school might not yield very comfortable answers, but being honest and warm with yourself about the things you do love about your role and your school should help to reframe the way you approach your work.

B. Listening schools

'The significant problems we face cannot be solved at the same level of thinking we were at when we created them.'

Albert Einstein

A huge part of the problem is the obsession with *doing*. We seem to think somehow that the more we *do*, the safer we are. The obsession with busyness is no more than a distraction at a time when we are in the middle of a crisis of purpose – a crisis we are only partially able to influence.

I think deep down, behind everything we do in life, there is a lurching feeling of insecurity and an existential struggle. I would argue at the moment that by 'doing' without thinking or acting in accordance with real values, we master no more than the art of distraction. When I spoke with Jamie Thom, I told him I thought there was a reason why his book resonated with so many people. It's counterintuitive, but the more I think about it, real integrity and credibility comes not only from choosing what to do, but choosing what *not* to do.

For me, at every level, reclamation is linked intrinsically to courage – the courage to listen to ourselves and what values we hold most dear, and the courage to live through those values every day. As we've seen, there are some truly inspirational educational leaders in this country who are doing this, and those with influence above and below them need to take heart from that and follow their lead. At the highest levels of government, leaders need to ask themselves what they can do to provide a platform for school leaders to take risks and associate rigour with love and warmth rather than fear and threat.

Education is about nurture and development. There is simply no way that we can expect to provide this for our young people if we do not know how to do this for ourselves and our colleagues. It's time we understood that we all have psychological needs that need to be met before we can perform at our best. The very *least* we can offer the young people in our schools is a primarily soothing environment that has a drive linked closely to values rather than outcomes. I'd argue that the current framework leaves us chasing our tails rather than thinking about how we can ensure teachers and young people feel truly valued and autonomous. Anything linked solely to extrinsic measures will be plagued in the long term – it doesn't matter if it's a lesson that teaches essay skills simply by providing sentence stems, a learning walk that judges staff solely on the presence of mini whiteboards, or a 'growth mindset school' that mentions it once then measures the success by what's on the walls. Even if a school achieves the results it thinks it needs to feel successful, what then? The same again next year? At best, schools trap themselves into cycles that become self-reinforcing and addictive. *It doesn't mean anything.*

How do we start? By *listening*. Dame Alison Peacock spoke of creating a 'listening school'. That, for me, is the key. We need to listen to ourselves and understand our own pain and suffering – whether it be fear or insecurity – before we begin to alleviate the suffering of those around us. Warm and unwavering honesty breeds integrity and credibility. Only when I really understood my own experience could I begin to understand the difficulties faced by those around me – both colleagues and students.

We are united by our ability to love, and our experience of suffering, both of which are fundamental to being human. It's time we recognised that. This is not possible through assuming deficit and incompetence, but through listening to stakeholders and understanding their points of departure, and what they need in order to succeed. True compassion has inhibitors – at both systemic and personal levels – which make it exceptionally difficult. But then again, true compassion captures the very essence of bravery.

I have complete confidence in asserting that this is the *only* way forward. Even if we begin to argue that accountability means we have to be 'on' people all the time – before, during or after the event – ultimately, being 'on' people is no guarantee of success, nor is it a sustainable model (as I've outlined above). How many schools out there claim not to do things for Ofsted, and then hide behind all of those policies and structures that we all know are geared for a dawn raid when that call comes? The threats we now perceive are hypothetical in nature, and they won't eat us – we're don't live in jungles anymore. Locating a problem within someone else is a remarkably easy means of distracting us away from our own insecurities and pain; and more seriously, this also provides a useful means of covering up our own integrity and credibility. I like what Mary Myatt told me when she said that we can only really look to others when we have been entirely honest with ourselves.

Being compassionate means recognising the difficulties we all face, and recognising that sometimes people just need to be *heard*, sometimes they need a *solution*, and sometimes they need both. It's a truth – maybe even an inconvenient one for some people – that we all need to acknowledge. Logistically, we can begin to create the space in our schools, classrooms and ourselves to allow this to happen. In some cases, this space needs to be a physical space for people to go in and *stop*. We know we need drive to be successful in schools, but which path have we taken to ensure success? Spaces and structures – whether that be a quiet room, a yoga class, a staff room with tea and biscuits, or protected time on a timetable – that give us time to stop and be mindful are not a threat to slow things up and give refuge to those who want to 'take advantage'.

What does a listening school look like, then? Of course, it starts from the top. A listening school should start by listening to *itself* and its staff. Just as the body can tell us all kinds of things about our health, so the behaviours and problems that emerge in the ecosystem of an organisation can indicate the fitness of that organisation. It doesn't take a genius to read the research undertaken in Section 2 and recognise that *good* people are starting to vote with their feet, and many left behind are plagued by a sense of apathy and a loss of agency. Becoming a listening school starts by being unwaveringly honest and self-aware of what needs to change and how we need to get there, and – shock horror – it may start with the people who have the most influence to make things better. A listening school combines drive with soothe in the most powerful way possible: by framing it with love. It starts when leaders acknowledge their own inhibitors of compassion and their own perceived threats. The threat of losing a job is *not* a justification for waving that threat at someone else. Threatening people with their careers or mortgage payments will achieve nothing.

It's not just about creating opportunities for people to be heard, but being the kind of leader that someone can always bring things to. Dame Alison Peacock, for example, recognised that she could not be the person to carry all of that on her own, so she created the space for herself and the structure in order to provide a means for people to be heard. This includes the wider community, and this might not yield the instant positive results you'd hope for – but as long as it's in accordance with our values, who cares? Good outcomes are a by-product of meaningfully lived-through values. Yes, authorities and wider powers that be need to acknowledge the difficulties and smaller margins for error in some communities, but that doesn't need to stop schools making the right choices.

C. What I hope you'll take away from this book

'Pay no attention to the man behind the curtain.'
The Wizard of Oz

1. Compassion isn't about self-pity; it's about warmth and honesty.

Love *is* the answer: love from those around you, and love for yourself. If nothing else, it can provide the incubator for us while we're vulnerable, and it shows us that all is not lost. The thoughts you might be plagued with are just thoughts; they aren't an intrinsic indication about any more than that your mind is telling you that it needs to cool off. I hope that Section 3 allowed you to understand that your thoughts, emotions, feelings and behaviour are part of a *cycle* – a cycle which isn't easily broken by a single piece of meditation. The cycle isn't meant to be broken, really. The cycle just needs to be noticed. My own experience with mental health opened the lid on my Pandora's box full of insecurity and self-doubt. And it became unbearable. I mentioned before that my own depression and anxiety isn't entirely gone; I don't think it will ever be. It just hurts less than it used to, and there will probably be times when it re-occurs, and when I will need help and support from those around me to gain that all-important perspective.

Fundamentally, we are all human, and we all have the same fate. We need to recognise that. I detest the rhetoric that circulates around some schools (probably more than some, actually): 'Oh yeah, he's crap; she's OK but arrogant; she's been going 30 years and doesn't listen.' There's nothing intrinsic about those statements: they are *judgements*. If you feel they may be being said about you, then – trust me – it doesn't *mean* anything. Being behind on your marking is every bit as much about the systems around you and the people you are working with as it is about yourself. So you might need a bit of development on planning and marking in order to make sure it's a bit smoother and more manageable? Everyone has things they need to work on, however well they might hide it. Never compare your insides to come else's outsides. Yes, there's times when we all need to dig in and notice the discomfort or higher level of exertion; but when this comes to *define* your experience of your working environment, that's when honesty and self-compassion comes in, and it might be time to ask yourself more serious questions about being there.

2. Listen to yourself and make time and space for the things that matter.

There is sound scientific evidence to support the idea that we thrive when we feel as if we have got time for the things that matter to us, and that we feel we matter too. True, some working environments will naturally allow this more than others, but that isn't the end of the story. It can be as small as enjoying a cup of tea, savouring a small success or just a 'good morning'. Mindfulness is *not* about sitting in a quiet place and humming; it is about being more aware of your experience – that can be the slowing of your breathing, or it can be simply noticing your own physical feelings or emotions as they occur. Basically, it's doing anything that reminds us that we are not robots, but sentient human beings. My own (wrong) gut reaction to the CFT model is that 'soothe' is somehow meek and mild, and will lose in the long run, in the same way that going to the gym is often the first thing off my list when I'm busy. But actually, soothe is the most powerful thing we have; it takes real courage of one's conviction to be soothing to yourself and others. It's no surprise when we hear that more troubled individuals have come from challenging circumstances; it's because they don't come from a position of love, safety and nurture. The effects of this are long term, and they are profound.

3. Discomfort and uncertainty are part of life.

Love is what makes us human, but it's also what makes us vulnerable. Not only this, but the view of happiness that we are force-fed is one of a destination that will somehow lead to nirvana. Unfortunately, accepting discomfort and uncertainty is a key dimension of self-compassion. Fortunately, accepting that very fact is empowering and can give us an opportunity and a space to learn about ourselves. What we perceive as discomfort and uncertainty is tricky: at times, the discomfort and uncertainty in our environments will be intolerable, and they will be due more to the environment you find yourself in; and sometimes, there will be more work we can do as individuals to find a healthy place to *be* psychologically in our schools. As you read this book, whatever your position, there will be things that you can and cannot control, and there always will be. In the meantime, being compassionate with yourself is the place to start, simply because you won't be beating yourself up for things which aren't true, and which you cannot really exert any influence over.

4. We all have a responsibility before change can happen.

Sound logic is sound logic, so there is no surprise that when one speaks to people like Mary Myatt, Dame Alison Peacock and Jill Berry, what they say will chime with one another. These people aren't advocates solely for any group of people; they believe firmly in the collective role we have in the education of young people. Starting with ourselves is important because it's profoundly empowering. Once we understand ourselves in relation to others, we can begin to find a way forward. It will also allow us – with complete integrity – to know when we can do no more to affect change. I don't believe charity starts at home; compassion does, though.

Key points:

- Reclamation is the theme which runs through this book.
- This includes reclaiming our own feelings around our profession and how to cope within it.
- A key to the future of schools is for them to begin to listen to themselves, their staff, their students and their wider communities.
- We all have a responsibility to make change happen. This, I think, is empowering.
- We have the opportunity to mould our own experiences of schools, irrespective of the immediate environment.

Section 6: Further reading

Below is a collection of some of the most crucial reading I've done to complete this book. Some of it is directly cited above, but *all* of it has been vital in spirit in terms of forming my approach to compassion and its place in education.

Section 1: The start of compassion

- I would thoroughly recommend Ruby Wax's *How to Be Human: The Manual*, in which she continually intertwines the views of a Buddhist monk and a neuroscientist, finding common lines of enquiry and solutions between the spiritual and the scientific. The similarities are startling and comforting in equal measure. Towards the end of the book there's also a number of wonderful strategies for adults and children to use for coping with a wide range of psychological difficulties.

- For a magnificent synthesis of studies on depression, I'd recommend Johann Hari's book *Lost Connections*, which is both eloquent and inspiring.

- If you'd like something which is utterly comprehensive in terms of a thorough understanding of depression and mental health issues, Andrew Solomon's *The Noonday Demon: An Anatomy of Depression* is breathtakingly brilliant. It'll take you a year to read it though!

- If you're interested in compassion-focused therapy, then the seminal work is by the man himself – Paul Gilbert. It's called *The Compassionate Mind*.

Section 2: Our threat-based context

- The NFER's publication on *Teacher Workforce Dynamics* is well worth a read for understanding current patterns and trends: www.bit.ly/2GKMnSg (Accessed 13th December 2018).
- The *Teacher Wellbeing* Index, published by the Education Support Partnership also provides a very clear overview of the current state of affairs when it comes to teacher well-being: www.bit.ly/2Uy4crz (Accessed 9th December 2018).
- I've thoroughly enjoyed reading Mary Myatt's Hopeful Schools and *High Challenge, Low Threat* – both of which are warm, insightful and full of wisdom.

Section 3: Compassionate relationships

- If you'd like to start to think more proactively about compassion-focused therapy, I would highly recommend *Experiencing Compassion-Focused Therapy from the Inside Out* by Russell Kolts and his colleagues.
- If you'd like to explore the practical applications of CFT further, then www.compassionatemind.co.uk is a wonderful website full of free resources for you to get started.
- The work of Mary Welford in terms of the application of CFT in schools is really worth reading, and it can be found here: www.bit.ly/2EbMEfy
- Mary has also written a book entitled *The Compassionate Mind Approach to Building Self-Confidence*, which is exceptional.

Section 4: Compassionate teaching

- Peps Mccrea's book *Memorable Teaching* is a work of genius. Nothing more to say on it. As a teacher, if you read nothing again in your life – ever – then this book is enough!
- Harry Fletcher-Wood's *Responsive Teaching* feels like the book that should have been written about assessment for learning at the outset.

- Daniel Willingham's *Why Don't Students Like School?* is comprehensive yet accessible when it comes to bringing cognition into the classroom.

- You probably won't find a better attempt to deconstruct the art of explanation than Andy Tharby's *How To Explain Absolutely Anything to Absolutely Anyone.*

- Alex Quigley's *Vocabulary Gap* already feels like it's going to be an incredibly important piece of work for a long time to come.

- In terms of methods to use in our classrooms which work, there's a reason why Doug Lemov's *Teach Like a Champion* has been so successful – there's plenty of strategies in there that will prove useful to teachers at all stages in their careers.

Bibliography

Benyohai, M. (2018) 'The difference between measuring progress and attainment', *Medium.com*. Available at: www.bit.ly/2N1SaUA (Accessed 15 Oct 2018).

Brown, G. W. and Harris, T. O. (2011) *Social origins of depression: a study of psychiatric disorder in women*. Abingdon: Routledge.

Children Welfare Information Gateway (2015) *Understanding the effects of maltreatment on brain development*. Washington, DC: US Department of Health and Human Services. Available at: www.bit.ly/2BuHmde (Accessed 12 Oct 2018).

The Compassionate Mind Foundation (no date) 'Scales', *The Compassionate Mind Foundation* [Online]. Available at: www.bit.ly/2trFA8f (Accessed 25 Oct 2018).

Didau, D. (2014) 'Closing the language gap: building vocabulary', *Learning Spy* [Online]. Available at: www.bit.ly/2tjG4x1 (Accessed 20 Oct 2018).

Didau, D. (2015) 'Using threshold concepts to design a KS4 English curriculum', *Learning Spy* [Online]. Available at: www.bit.ly/2WTjIjA (Accessed 20 Oct 2018).

Dix, P. (2017) *When the adults change, everything changes*. Carmarthen: Crown House Publishing Ltd.

Education Support Partnership (2018) *Teacher wellbeing index 2018*. Available at: www.bit.ly/2Uy4crz (Accessed 24 Oct 2018).

Flanagan, M. (2018) 'Threshold concepts: undergraduate teaching, postgraduate training, professional development and school education', *Michael Thomas Flanagan's Home Page* [Online]. Available at: www.bit. ly/2E9lXYM (Accessed 20 Oct 2018).

Fletcher-Wood, H. (2018) *Responsive teaching*. Abingdon: Routledge.

FORA.tv (2010) *The golden circle: why does Apple command loyalty?* [Video]. Available at: www.bit.ly/2Eiq8kU (Accessed 4 Oct 2018).

'Forgetting Curve', *The SAGE Glossary of the Social and Behavioral Sciences*, www.bit.ly/2N1T5Ew.

Gilbert, P. (2006) 'Evolution and depression: issues and implications', *Psychological Medicine* 36 (3) pp. 287–297.

Gilbert, P. (2009) 'Introducing compassion-focused therapy', *Advances in Psychiatric Treatment* 15 (3) pp. 199–208.

Gilbert, P. (2014) 'The origins and nature of compassion focused therapy', *British Journal of Clinical Psychology* 53 (1) pp. 6–41.

Gilbert, P. (2015) *The compassionate mind: a new approach to life's challenges*. London: Constable & Robinson.

Hampton, D. (2015) 'What's the difference between feelings and emotions?', *The Best Brain Possible* [blog]. Available at: www.bit. ly/2MROuox (Accessed 31 Mar 2018).

Hari, J. (2018) *Lost connections: uncovering the real causes of depression – and the unexpected solutions*. London: Bloomsbury.

Hawkley, L. C. and Cacioppo, J. T. (2011) 'Perceived social isolation: social threat vigilance and its implications for health' in Decety, J. and Cacioppo, J. T. (eds) *The Oxford handbook of social neuroscience*. Oxford: Oxford University Press, pp. 765–775.

Holleran, G. (no date) *Teachers' Mental Health and Wellness* [Online]. Available at: www.teachersmentalhealthandwellness.com (Accessed 15 Oct 2018).

Johnson, E. A. and O'Brien, K. A. (2013) 'Self-compassion soothes the savage ego-threat system: effects on negative affect, shame, rumination, and depressive symptoms', *Journal of Social and Clinical Psychology* 32 (9) pp. 939–963.

Killian, S. (2017) 'Hattie's 2017 updated list of factors influencing student achievement', *EvidenceBasedTeaching.org.au*. Available at: www. bit.ly/2T6tHmw (Accessed Oct 4 2018).

Kolts, R. L., Irons, C., Bell, T., Bennett-Levy, J. and Gilbert, P. (2018) *Experiencing compassion-focused therapy from the inside out: a self-practice/self-reflection workbook for therapists.* New York, NY: Guilford Press.

Lemov, D. (2010) *Teach like a champion.* San Francisco, CA: Jossey-Bass.

Marmot, M. (2015) *Status syndrome: how your social standing directly affects your health.* London: Bloomsbury.

Mccrea, P. (2017) *Memorable teaching: leveraging memory to build deep and durable learning in the classroom.* Scotts Valley, CA: CreateSpace Independent Publishing Platform.

Myatt, M. (2016a) *High challenge, low threat: finding the balance.* Woodbridge: John Catt Educational Ltd.

Myatt, M. (2016b) *Hopeful schools: building humane communities.* London: Mary Myatt Learning Limited.

Nummenmaa, L., Glerean, E., Hari, R. and Hietanen, J. K. (2014) 'Bodily maps of emotions', *Proceedings of the National Academy of Sciences* 111 (2) pp. 646–651.

Ofsted (2018) *Ofsted inspections: myths.* Department for Education. Available at: www.bit.ly/2EbWjTn (Accessed 18 Oct 2018).

Ofsted and Spielman, A. (2018) *Amanda Spielman speech to the SCHOOLS NorthEast summit* [Transcript]. Available at: www.gov.uk/government/speeches/amanda-spielman-speech-to-the-schools-northeast-summit (Accessed 11 Oct 2018).

Padesky, C. A. and Mooney, K. A. (1990) 'Presenting the cognitive model to clients', *International Cognitive Therapy Newsletter* 6 (1) pp. 13–14.

Pink, D. (2011) *Drive: the surprising truth about what motivates us.* Edinburgh: Canongate Books.

Preidt, R. (2017) 'Loneliness may lead to sleepless nights', *WebMD* [Online]. Available at: www.bit.ly/2DS4V12 (Accessed 6 Oct 2018).

Quigley, A. (2018) *Closing the vocabulary gap.* Abingdon: Routledge.

Rosenshine, B. (2012) 'Principles of instruction: research-based strategies that all teachers should know', *American Educator* 36 (1) pp. 12–19, 39. Available at: www.bit.ly/2SxqbSN (Accessed 18 Oct 2018).

Schofield, K. and Bates, L. (2018) 'Philip Hammond says extra budget cash for schools was "nice gesture" following backlash', *PoliticsHome* [Online]. Available at: www.bit.ly/2TmwIMz (Accessed 1 Nov 2018).

Sherrington, T. (2017) '10 low impact activities to do less of – or stop altogether', *Teacherhead* [Blog]. Available at: www.bit.ly/2GaRuLk (Accessed 5 Oct 2018).

Sherrington, T. (2017) *The learning rainforest.* Woodbridge: John Catt Educational Ltd.

Sherrington, T. (2015) 'Behaviour management: a Bill Rogers top 10', *Teacherhead* [blog]. Available at: www.bit.ly/2DulcrQ (Accessed 12 Oct 2018).

Sherrington, T. (2018) 'How can we measure and report progress meaningfully?', *Teacherhead* [blog]. Available at: www.bit.ly/2N2mvmd (Accessed 15 Oct 2018).

Simon-Thomas, E. R., Godzik, J., Castle, E., Antonenko, O., Ponz, A., Kogan, A. and Keltner, D. J. (2012) 'An fMRI study of caring vs self-focus during induced compassion and pride', *Social Cognitive and Affective Neuroscience* 7 (6) pp. 635–648.

Staufenberg, J. (2017) 'Revealed: the "sausage-machine schools" pushing new teachers out the profession', *Schools Week* [Online]. Available at: www.bit.ly/2sTlBz9 (Accessed 5 Oct 2018).

Teacher Development Trust (2018) 'What is lesson study?', *Teacher Development Trust* [Online]. Available at: www.bit.ly/2X0hFu5 (Accessed 20 Oct 2018).

Tharby, A. (2018) *How to explain absolutely anything to absolutely anyone.* Carmarthen: Crown House Publishing Ltd.

Tomasello, M. and Vaish, A. (2013) 'Origins of human cooperation and horality', *Annual Review of Psychology* 64 (1) pp. 231–255.

Wax, R. (2018) *How to be human: the manual.* London: Penguin Life.

Welford, M. (2012) *The compassionate mind approach to building your self-confidence.* London: Constable & Robinson.

Welford, M. and Langmead, K. (2015) 'Compassion-based initiatives in educational settings', *Educational and Child Psychology* 32 (1) pp. 71–80.

Wiliam, D. (2018) *Embedded formative assessment.* Bloomington, IN: Solution Tree Press.

Willingham, D. T. (2010) *Why don't students like school?* San Francisco, CA: Jossey-Bass.

Worth, J., Lynch, S., Hillary, J., Rennie, C. and Andrade, J. (2018) *Teacher workforce dynamics in England.* Slough: National Foundation for Educational Research. Available at: www.bit.ly/2EmdhOP (Accessed 4 Nov 2018).